I.S.A.M. Monographs: Number 19

Ives:
A Survey of the Music

H. WILEY HITCHCOCK

I.S.A.M. Monographs: Number 19

Ives:
A Survey of the Music

H. WILEY HITCHCOCK

Institute for Studies in American Music
Conservatory of Music
Brooklyn College
of The City University of New York

Copyright © Oxford University Press, 1977
First published in the Oxford Studies of Composers (14) by
Oxford University Press, London, 1977
Reprinted, with corrections, by arrangement with Oxford University Press,
  New York
Library of Congress Catalogue No. 83-081307
ISBN 0-914678-21-3
Printed in the United States of America

An asterisk in the margin refers the reader to an item in the Corrigenda, p. 96.

Published by Institute for Studies in American Music
Conservatory of Music
Brooklyn College of the City University of New York
Brooklyn, New York 11210

To John Kirkpatrick

FOREWORD

CHARLES Ives was born on 20 October 1874 in Danbury, Connecticut, in the rolling, wooded land of southwestern New England. He descended from old Anglo-American stock. The greatest influence on his life, his thought, and his music was that of his * father George Ives, Danbury's principal musician, a versatile instrumentalist, conductor, and musical arranger who had a uniquely open mind about musical possibilities and experimented constantly with unconventional tone systems and instruments. He gave his son Charles a thorough grounding in traditional (and nontraditional) music theory and a lasting love and respect for the American vernacular music of hymns, popular and traditional songs and dances, ragtime, brass bands, and theatre orchestras. Ives attended Yale University from 1894 to 1898, studying there with Horatio Parker, eminent figure among the German-trained 'Second New England School' of academic composers who had no truck with American vernacular music, seeking inspiration rather in the art music of the European Classic-Romantic tradition.

Ives's eclectic, individualistic, and radical works found almost no sympathetic performers or listeners; although his vocation was clearly to musical composition and he was a church organist from 1889 to 1902, he decided to give up a career as professional musician for one in the insurance business. This he pursued with great success from 1898 until his retirement in 1930. Meanwhile, the onset of World War I, a severe heart attack in 1918, profound disillusionment with the results of the American elections of November 1920, and—perhaps most fundamentally—the strain of his double life and the rejection by others of his music had virtually ended Ives's composing: few works postdate 1921, which saw a final burst of songs.

Between 1902 (when he resigned from his last organist's job) and 1920 there had not been a single performance of Ives's music generated by anyone's efforts besides his own. His private printings between 1919 and 1922 of the Second Piano Sonata ('Concord'), a book of *Essays Before a Sonata*, and a volume of *114 Songs* were the first steps toward the diffusion of his music beyond a tiny circle of family and friends. But it was not for many years that it gradually began to be heard, let alone accepted or prized, on any significant scale; and essentially, the current view of Ives as America's first great composer (some would say its greatest) dates only since World War II.

Since no general survey of Ives's music has been published, it has seemed worth the effort to attempt one, even in a book that must necessarily be very brief. Hence the organization of this volume according to the principal genres in which Ives worked. But this organization also reflects the fact that Ives's compositional career, lasting roughly from 1890 to 1925, did not follow a clear-cut line of development chronologically. Not only would it be difficult to define 'periods' in that career, as one can with composers like Beethoven or Stravinsky, but one cannot really generalize about 'the Ives style'; stylistic pluralism was characteristic of his music almost from the beginning. Simple and complex, traditional and radical, conventional and experimental, homespun and rarefied, spiritual and slapstick—these and many other dichotomies jostle each other in neighbourly fashion throughout his life as a composer. So too do modes of musical expression derived from widely varied sources. Ives was explicit about the inclusiveness with which he embraced the whole sonorous world that he knew or could imagine as potential raw material for his music: 'The fabric of existence weaves itself whole. . . . There can be nothing "*exclusive*" about a substantial art.'[1] Thus his music has roots not only in that of the masters (and lesser composers) of European and American art music and in the friendly vernacular traditions of his native New England (hymn tunes, country fiddling, camp-meeting songs, brass-band marches, piano rags, patriotic and popular ditties, songs of hearth and home) but also in 'unmusical' sounds—horses' hooves on cobblestones, out-of-tune volunteer church choirs, the

[1] Quoted first in Henry Bellamann, 'Charles Ives; the Man and his Music', *Musical Quarterly*, xix (1933), pp. 45–58.

crack of bat and ball, the special quality of 'a horn over a lake', the clash of two bands at opposite sides of a town square each playing its own march in its own tempo—and in untried sounds as well—harmonies in massed seconds or other novel stacks of intervals, microtones, tone-rows, rhythmic and metric serialism, unique instrumental combinations.

*   *   *   *

This study relies much on the three main sources of documentation for Ives's music and his writings about it: John Kirkpatrick's catalogue of Ives's manuscripts and his edition of Ives's *Memos* (dictated in 1932) and Howard Boatwright's edition of Ives's *Essays Before a Sonata, The Majority and Other Writings*. (Full citations of these will be found in the 'Selective Bibliography' at the end of this volume, and grateful thanks are due to W. W. Norton & Co., Inc., for permission to quote from the latter two.) Quotations from the *Memos* or the *Essays* are noted parenthetically as such in the body of the text; quotations from Ives's manuscript marginalia derive from Kirkpatrick's catalogue, under the entries for the works to which they relate, unless indicated otherwise.

The dedication of this book is acknowledgment of the enormous debt owed by me (as by all other students of Ives) to the artistry, the scholarship, and the generosity and grace of spirit of John Kirkpatrick, to whom is due even the possibility of viewing Ives's music in the round. Students in my Brooklyn College and City University of New York seminars have contributed many valuable insights, especially Carol Baron, Carl Skoggard, Laurie Spiegel, Judith Tick, Jodi Vogel, and Robin Warren. Four others to whom I am especially grateful for having read and criticized the book in draft form are Janet Hitchcock, Sidney Cowell, Iain Fenlon, and Vivian Perlis.

Florence
December 1975

CONTENTS

1. THE SONGS

IVES's songs make a good point of departure for a survey of his music. They span his life as a composer: his earliest known work (*Slow March*; ?1887) and his last completed one (*Sunrise*; 1926) are songs; in between, he wrote about 150 others, most of which he gathered into the book of *114 Songs*. In the songs we meet the immense diversity of compositional manner and material—the inclusiveness—that characterizes Ives's work as a whole; also its range, from the miniature to the mighty, the ultra-simple to the bewilderingly complex, the comic to the profound. To begin with the songs, moreover, is to affirm that the very foundation of Ives's musical personality was a melodic gift of grace and power.

Ives is notorious as a radical pathfinder who arrived—alone, virtually uninfluenced (except by his father)—at modes of musical expression that other composers of international stature exploited systematically only later. But he remained in many ways a late nineteenth-century American, a product of that era termed by Lewis Mumford 'the brown decades'. The subject matter of Ives's works is overwhelmingly retrospective: memories of boyhood life in a New England country town. And the kind of song he wrote in greatest numbers is the 'household song' of sentiment, voicing some emotion of affection, nostalgia, or yearning; pleasant to perform and to hear, and not too demanding technically. It had been a favourite American genre for a long time; Stephen Foster's songs for the parlour were neither the first nor the last of the sort. Practically all of Ives's early songs are in this vein, beginning with *Slow March*, composed at age 12 or 13, a gentle account of the burial of a family pet (Ex. 1).

Ives's borrowing of the 'Dead March' from Handel's *Saul* for the introduction (and also the epilogue) of *Slow March* is the first instance of his lifelong practice of musical 'quotation'; more than 150 tunes have been identified as such in his works, mainly traditional American hymn tunes, popular and patriotic songs, marches, and ragtime strains but also themes from Handel, Bach, Beethoven, Brahms, Foster, and other composers. Ives's quoting or otherwise re-using extant music (sometimes his own) has been much discussed, perhaps mainly because the practice, once as much a commonplace in music (e.g. in Renaissance chansons, motets, and

Used by permission (see page 98).

Masses) as in the graphic arts or literature, had fallen into disuse by the nineteenth century, or was exploited self-consciously, often with programmatic or nationalistic aims. But Ives's 'quotations' have nothing to do with nationalism, folklorism, or mere local colour. Like those of Joyce, Pound, or Picasso, they were as natural to him as pure invention: the pre-existent melodies that so often figure in his compositions were simply part of his auditory experience, just as susceptible to reworking into an artistic present as the storehouse in memory of a novelist or poet, or the visual experience (whether of nature or prior art) of a painter. Of course the tunes that Ives borrowed had associations for him, but his use of them usually goes far beyond mere associative value. Borrowed melodies are sometimes the very basis of the musical fabric, and they are treated variously, from the baldest verbatim quotations of single tunes or collage-like assemblages of them to the most subtle cloudy allusions, reminiscences, and half-rememberings. In *The Things Our Fathers Loved* (1917), for example, bits of six American popular songs are quoted, and in *He Is There!* (1917) snatches of no fewer than thirteen pre-existent tunes appear. On the other hand, in *Down East* (1919) a dreamy chromatic introduction gives way to a tantalizingly familiar, homespun melody (Ex. 2); only

near the close of the song does Ives actually quote precisely Lowell Mason's hymn tune *Bethany* ('Nearer, my God, to Thee'), revealing it (Ex. 3) as the nostalgic, pervasive source of the entire composition.

Many of Ives's mature songs, though clearly in the tradition of the household song, transcend its usual technical and artistic limitations by carefully-wrought details of style. In *Two Little Flowers* (1921) the vocal melody, having begun almost predictably in smooth contours of pitch and rhythm, is interrupted by three tiny rhythmic jolts (marked 'x' in Ex. 4). These highlight in a subtle way the syntactical divisions of the verses, and they prepare the wholly original climax, at which the line traverses a downward tenth to pause suspensively on 'all' (unless the singer cannot make it; and Ives offers an easier alternative, in the kind of gesture to practical expediency that characterizes much of his music). Similar rhythmic disruptions punctuate the ends of each half of *At the River* and of *Serenity* (see Ex. 14).

Ives was not above parodying the household song, for he detested the banality, morbidity, and maudlin sentimentality (as opposed

Ex.4

to genuine sentiment) that had traditionally marked the genre. One of his most devilish 'take-offs' (his term for parodies, sometimes implying a hint, or more than a hint, of wicked satire) is *On the Counter* (1920). Its text (by Ives) is a derisive sneer at 'the same old chords, the same old time, the same old sentimental sound', its
* music a cracked-mirror reflection of Ethelbert Nevin's, ending with a rueful quotation of *Auld Lang Syne* after teasingly leaving the parodied composer's name to be supplied by the singer (Ex. 5).

Ex. 5

If the household song is at the core of Ives's lyric art, other types of song are part of it as well. These fall into three groups: songs that spring from the bedrock of American vernacular-tradition music; songs based on radical experiments in tonal or rhythmic organization; and songs that share the aspirations, and usually the abstract, non-associative musical language, of the Euro-American art-song tradition.

The vernacular tradition of American music is the source of such purposeful pleasantries as the group in *114 Songs* that Ives called '5 Street Songs and Pieces' (*Old Home Day, In the Alley, A Son of a Gambolier*, and *The Circus Band*, besides *Down East*)- and of the nostalgic, Sunday-morning group of '4 Songs Based on Hymntune Themes' (*Watchman, At the River, His Exaltation*, and *The Camp Meeting*). There is a manuscript sketch dating from Ives's first year at Yale (1894) for the brassy march music of *The Circus Band* (the words came later); the same year, perhaps even earlier, Ives worked up a popular dance tune, *Little Annie Rooney*, into the rollicking wedding song, *Waltz*. He adapted *A Son of a Gambolier* (1895) from two earlier piano marches he had written; in it he quotes a traditional melody (of Irish origin?) and near the end invites the improvisatory participation of a 'Kazoo Chorus[:]

Flutes, fiddles and flageolets . . . [then] add piccolos, ocarinas and fifes'. Similarly, *Old Home Day* (?1913) has a 'Chorus' in which instruments long associated with popular and amateur music-making are invited optionally to play along: 'Obligato (ad lib) fife, violin or flute'.

The four hymn-tune songs exemplify Ives's lifelong practice of revising, rearranging, adapting, or recomposing earlier works. All four derived from instrumental pieces. *Watchman* (1913), based on a tune by Mason, was taken from the last movement of the First Violin Sonata (the *Watchman* sections of which were themselves adaptations from a setting of 1901, now lost, for soprano and organ); it was to reappear, recomposed, as the first movement of the Fourth Symphony. *At the River* (?1916) came from the third movement of the Fourth Violin Sonata; *His Exaltation* (1913) from the first movement of the Second Violin Sonata; and *The Camp Meeting* (1912) from various parts of the Third Symphony's last * movement that use the hymn tune *Azmon*.

Popular-music idioms inform many other songs as well. The transcendental text of *Walking* (1900–?2) mentions 'a roadhouse, a dance going on' (to be spoken, if voiced at all), and the piano launches into an interlude in ragtime rhythms (Ex. 6). Spoken text is explicitly demanded in the central climax of the cowboy ballad

Ex.6

Charlie Rutlage (1920/21)—or, rather than spoken text, an original kind of *Sprechstimme* (Ives had not heard or seen Schoenberg's kind) in which the vocal rhythm but not the pitches is notated. At the beginning and the end of the song, guitar-like strumming accompanies the voice, and Ives's setting of the colloquialisms of the poetry is so sensitive that it is difficult to sing it with anything but the appropriate drawling accent of the American Southwest. Example 7 shows the transition from the peak of the recited section

back to the music 'as in the beginning'. Ives's footnote is a re-
minder of one of his most startling statements—'My God! What has
sound got to do with music!' (*Essays* 84)—and the piano part to
which it refers is a powerful example of his use of tone-clusters
toward expressive ends.

Ex. 7

A kind of musical deadpan humour shines through the brief song
on lower Manhattan's impudent little two-block-long *Ann Street*
and the lurching merry-go-round music of *The Side Show*
(both 1921). Childlike music in skipping rhythms related to children's play-party songs appears in both the early *Memories* (1897)
and the late *The Greatest Man* (1921). Akin to popular American
songs in their texts' concern with topical social and political issues
—virtually musical editorials—are *Nov. 2, 1920* or *The Election*

15

(1921), which begins with the homespun line 'It strikes me that . . .';
Majority (1921), on a humanitarian theme so central to Ives's
thinking that he gave the song the place of honour as No. 1 in
114 Songs; and '3 Songs of the War' (*In Flanders Fields, He Is
There!*, and *Tom Sails Away*; all 1917), their music a network of
popular and patriotic tunes from the American past and present.

To turn directly from Ives's songs of popular inspiration to
those of radical musical organization is to reaffirm the scope of his
musical vocabulary and the open-mindedness, the inclusiveness, of
his musical attitudes as well as his inventiveness, daring, and
visionary reach.

In *Like a Sick Eagle* (?1909) not only are both melody and harmony so chromatic as to be virtually atonal but Ives suggests that
the voice slide from note to note (in a line moving mostly by semitones) through quarter-tones, as a violin had done in the original
chamber-orchestra version. Wholly unbarred, the song has a steady
underlying pulse in quavers that is organized by the voice into long
serpentine phrases, no two of the same length and all set off against
shorter, asymmetrical groupings in the accompaniment. Thus the
music is projected on two planes seemingly quite independent of
each other. Similarly unbarred, 'atonal', and on two planes is *The
Cage* (arranged in 1906 from a chamber work of the same year).
Its background chords are built up by perfect fourths and fifths;
the foreground melody moves mostly by whole-tones. Said Ives:
'Technically this piece is but a study of how chords of 4ths and 5ths
may throw melodies away from a set tonality. . . . [The] principal
thing in this movement is to show that a song does not necessarily
have to be in any one key to make musical sense. To make music in
no particular key has a nice name nowadays [1932] —"atonality".'
(*Memos* 55–6) ('Nice', in Ives's vocabulary, was a particularly
damning epithet, meaning conventional, conformist, meek, and
weak.)

Mists (1910), set to a lovely poem by Ives's wife, Harmony
Twichell, on the death of her mother, has three or four planes
depending on how one listens. One is the grateful, shapely vocal
melody, another the tolling bell of the bass. Between these is a
gently oscillating stream of misty augmented triads, which is
shadowed high in the piano register by a similar stream that should
be 'scarcely audible'. This 'shadow' (a favourite concept of Ives) is
like a distant choir humming heterophonically along with the
middle plane, or like a mirror-reflection of it seen from afar (Ex. 8).

16

Ex. 8

Such visual and spatial analogies as these often leap to mind in hearing Ives's planar, heterophonic polyphony, and well they might, for he thought in such terms:

A natural procedure in a piece of music, be it a song or a week's symphony, may have something in common [with] a walk up a mountain. There's the mountain, its foot, its summit—there's the valley—the climber looks, turns, and looks down or up. He sees the valley, but not exactly the same angle he saw it at [in] the last look—and the summit is changing with every step—and the sky. (*Memos* 196)

This notion, mildly as Ives puts it, was in fact one of his most radical, and it is an important key to much of his music, which is often a multi-faceted, multi-layered—indeed, multi-dimensional—microcosm in which individual objects or events co-exist, each maintaining its individuality yet influencing and being influenced by the others. Ives viewed such a co-existence as no more threatening to 'order' in music than, say, the co-existence in a forest of trees, rocks, mosses, flowers, animals, and insects is threatening to order; 'order' is here an irrelevant concept, or one too narrowly conceived.

Ives's layered polyphony is sometimes so dense, the relationships between its co-existing events sometimes so subtle and their sequence so apparently haphazard and unplanned, that it can seem chaotic even through many listenings. But that Ives's musical thought was 'chaotic' is belied by his not infrequently turning to 'pre-compositional' plans which are then pursued, with some rigour, in a work. Paradoxically, the result of such plans—themselves anything but chaotic—is often so unusual and knotty in sound that the ear fails to hear the logic and perceives even this carefully ordered music as bordering on chaos. In the late song *On the Antipodes* (1915–23) Ives may have intended to exploit this paradox. The poem is about the paradoxical ('antipodal') extremes of Nature: 'Nature's relentless; Nature is kind. Nature is Eternity; Nature's today! . . .' The music, for soprano or chorus and two pianos with optional organ at the close, is in disjunct sections which mirror the extremes of Nature expressed in the text. At beginning, centre, and end, however, the song is anchored by a recurrent series of giant chords, each made up systematically of different stacks of superimposed intervals. The sequence of these chords is carefully planned: from an opening sonority built up by perfect fifths, others of successively smaller stacked intervals appear, until one of crushed-together semitones is reached; then the process is reversed, and the sequence ends (as it had begun) with an immense chord of fifths. In Ex. 9, the last section of the song, the structural

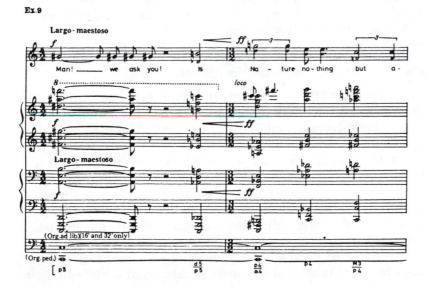

Ex. 9

18

basis of these chords is indicated beneath the music: p = perfect,* d = diminished, a = augmented, M = major, and m = minor. The final, strident, frustrated question of the poet (Ives) is expressed through a vocal line that leaps through a series of jagged intervals.

This line is not haphazard either: not only is it a twelve-note series, it is a carefully structured set of permutations of a three-note cell spanning a major third, with an inner minor third (Ex. 10). (The second vocal part, to be sung if the work is performed chorally, follows another twelve-note series.)

Ex.10

Another song, *Soliloquy*, is better known for this kind of proto-serialism, perhaps because of its hinting subtitle: '. . . a Study in 7ths and Other Things'. Its text, like that of *On the Antipodes* (and also by Ives), is about man's ambivalence before Nature:

> When a man is sitting before the fire on the hearth,
>   he says, 'Nature is a simple affair.'
> Then he looks out the window and sees a hailstorm,
>   and he begins to think that 'Nature can't be so
>   easily disposed of!'

The first verse is set almost monotonously as a drawling recitative over harmonies slowly swinging back and forth above a bass moving from d♭ to D♮ (i.e. a seventh). The second verse is a contrast in every way—tumultuous, frantic, stormy. The voice races chromatically in very wide intervals (the first phrase containing all twelve notes without repetition). The piano rushes similarly, first through arpeggios built of major sevenths (or minor ninths), then through chords built, like those of *On the Antipodes*, on varying structural intervals. A midpoint is reached, then everything is repeated in retrograde, including the sequence of bar-lengths (5, 6, 7, 8, and 5 semiquavers to the midpoint, then 5, 8, 7, 6, and 5), and also by inversion (arpeggios up in first half, down in second).

Soliloquy dates from 1907; thus it anticipates similar uses of twelve-note material, wide-spanned vocal melody emphasizing sevenths and ninths, and techniques of retrograde and inversion in the works of the Viennese school. Also prophetic, but anticipating rather the polytonal techniques of Stravinsky, Milhaud, and others, is an even earlier work, the *Song for Harvest Season* (1893), one of two youthful 'fugues in four keys'. In this song, scored for soprano with either organ or brass trio accompaniment, Ives explores the possibilities of imitative counterpoint in which bass, tenor, alto,

and soprano voices are respectively and consistently in C, F, B♭,*
and E♮.

   If the songs just discussed reveal the experimental, 'radical', and
prophetic side of Ives, another group is more unambiguously
within the tradition of art song based on texts of some poetic ele-
gance. At Yale, Horatio Parker habitually assigned well-known
song texts to be newly set by his students; Ives set a number while
at the university, more later. Thus there are Lieder by him—e.g.
Widmung (Müller) and *Die Lotosblume* and *Ich grolle nicht* (both
Heine)—and *mélodies* as well, e.g. *Chanson de Florian* and *Rosa-*   *
munde (Bélanger). Comparisons with European composers' earlier
settings are not always to Ives's disadvantage: he had learnt well
his models (Schubert, Schumann, Brahms; Massenet, Godard), as
the graceful first period of *Feldeinsamkeit* (1897) can suggest
(Ex. 11).

English and American poets of distinction tended to evoke from Ives settings of considerable complexity and strength (two qualities he usually equated), as in *A Farewell to Land* (Byron), *Requiem* (R. L. Stevenson), *From 'Lincoln, the Great Commoner'* (Edwin Markham), *From 'The Swimmers'* (L. Untermeyer), *Walt Whitman* (Whitman), or *From 'Paracelsus'* (Browning). On the other hand, among the most hauntingly tender and gentle of Ives's songs are *Evening* (1921; Milton), *Maple Leaves* (1920; T. B. Aldrich), and

Ex.12

Serenity (1919; Whittier). All three have delicious details of text-setting. In *Evening*, one may point to the perfect match between speech-like rhythm and grateful melodic arcs (Ex. 12a) and the utterly tranquil conclusion (Ex. 12b), with crystalline notes high in the piano suggesting the 'wakeful nightingale' of Milton's verses; 'conclusion' may be the wrong word, for the song really does not end, it simply fades away. *Maple Leaves* ends with delicate falling sequences in the voice which lead to a final phrase that flutters down like the autumn leaves of the title (Ex. 13). In *Serenity*, two

Ex. 13

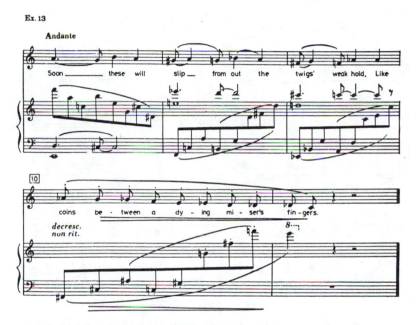

chords related to the cloudy mélange of distant bell tones, as unique and unforgettable as Wagner's '*Tristan* chord', oscillate high above the 'unison chant' of the voice part. Ives breaks this ostinato twice, releasing the slight tension built up by the sinuous chant and pointing up the ends of Whittier's stanzas; and he precedes the last word of each stanza with a catch-breath that lends a subtle emphasis, underscoring the two basic founts of serenity, love and peace (Ex. 14).

Ex. 14

Very slowly

Je - sus knelt to share with Thee, the si - lence of e - ter - ni - ty

In - ter - pre - ted by love. Take

from our souls the strain and stress, and let our or - dered lives con - fess, the

beau - ty of thy peace.

It is unfair to Ives to single out one song as his greatest, but the biggest and most dramatic, and one which synthesizes various sources of his lyric art, is *General William Booth Enters Into Heaven* (1914). This is a setting of portions of Vachel Lindsay's poem celebrating the militant revivalism of the first commanding general of the Salvation Army—a 'Glory trance', Ives once called it. Much of the song is march-like, and it begins and ends with a typical marching band's drumbeat (Ex. 15). The whack of snare drums and the thud of a bass drum limping a bit behind are embodied in dissonant clusters of a sort Ives had invented when, as a boy, he practised on a piano the drum parts he was to play in his father's band.[1] In various guises and transformations this kind of sonority pervades *General Booth*.

Ex. 15

[1] '[I] got to trying out sets of notes to go with or take-off the drums. . . . A popular chord in the right hand was . . . one with two white notes with the thumb, having the little finger run into a 7th or octave-and-semitone over the lower thumb note'

Lindsay's poem has Booth leading a noisy company of the blind and the leprous, of convicts, social misfits, and outcasts, through the gates of heaven. As they circle the 'court-house square' Jesus appears, stretching out his hands over the mob to heal and purge them; suddenly, they are 'spotless, clad in raiment new', and they march off into the distance. Their refrain throughout is a line from a Salvation Army hymn: 'Are you washed in the blood of the Lamb?' Ives chose not to set this line to the tune usually associated with it but to a different one derived from Lowell Mason's hymn *Cleansing Fountain* (Ex. 16). As is often true in Ives's works that are based on pre-existent tunes, his early references to the source are fragmentary and allusive; only late in the song does he offer a clear and more or less complete statement of it.

Ex. 16   Cleansing Fountain

Lindsay includes in his poem interlinear instrumental suggestions which Ives takes into account: heading the poem is the instruction 'Bass drum beaten loudly', on which Ives elaborates, as we have seen; at a mention of 'banjos' Ives quotes the beginning of James A. Bland's song *Oh, Dem Golden Slippers!*, composed for minstrel shows (with which the banjo was associated); and where Lindsay calls for a 'blare, blare' of trumpets, Ives introduces the military bugle-call *Reveille*. At the moment of transfiguration, when Jesus appears, Lindsay suggests 'sweet flute music'. Ives responds with a passage of moving tenderness (Ex. 17) in which the singer circles 'round and round' on a three-note figure, the pianist's right hand circles similarly but in a two-note cycle, while in the middle of the accompaniment, strangely askew metrically and rhythmically, the melody of *Cleansing Fountain* winds its tranquil

---

(*Memos* 42–3). Ives's next comments suggest how such 'imitative dissonance' led naturally to a general preference for complex, non-traditional harmonic materials: 'What started as a boy's play and in fun, gradually worked into something that had a serious side to it that opened up possibilities—and in ways sometimes valuable, as the ears got used to and acquainted with these various and many dissonant combinations. I remember distinctly, after this habit became a matter of years, that going back to the usual consonant triads, chords, etc., something strong seemed more or less missing. . . .'

way. The healing complete, the crowd marches off, singing triumphantly. (Ives here and there writes in an extra voice part, inviting

Ex.17

choral performance if desired.) The song ends with a haunting, off-key version of the refrain, set to hymnbook harmony; then the drumbeats, lower-pitched as if in the distance, fade—'as a band marching away', wrote Ives in the manuscript.

2. THE CHORAL MUSIC

FOR more than thirteen years from the time the *Danbury News* reported (on his birthday in 1888) that he was 'the youngest organist in the state', Ives was a church organist and, as such, a
* composer of church music. However, after his decision to go into business in 1902, he resigned his post at Central Presbyterian Church in New York City and shortsightedly (as it turned out) left much music there; all this was apparently thrown out when the church changed sites in 1915. The loss—of choral works as well as church solos and organ compositions—is sad, for the choral music by Ives that remains includes works of high and fresh quality. They fall into three groups: sacred works, most of which date from Ives's years on the organ bench and in choir lofts; partsongs, only a few of which, from the Yale years, remain; and other secular works, virtually all of which postdate the turn of the century.

What is amazing among the early sacred choruses is the imaginative stylistic leap Ives made between several compositions preserved from the early 1890s and a group of psalm settings made probably in the summer of 1894. In the two anthems *Turn Ye, Turn Ye* (?1890) and *Crossing the Bar* (?1891) there is hardly a hint that Ives was to become an 'irregular' as a composer. Both are well-crafted, pleasant pieces, but in a conventional church style that later generations rejected as too sweet to be powerful and too predictable to be exciting. Ives listed his having composed some twenty-odd such works 'alla Harry Rowe Shelley and Dudley Buck' (both of them Connecticut organist-composers with whom he studied while at Yale). The more expansive *Easter Carol* (1892; revised ?1901) is stronger but still squarely in the Victorian anthem tradition.

The series of psalm settings is another matter altogether. Since Ives wrote of his father's having tried them with the Danbury choirs, they must predate the fall of 1894 (when George Ives died).

Ives's recollection was that they included settings of Psalms 67, 150, 54, perhaps 24, and part of Psalm 90.

Best known, probably because it was the first to be published and recorded (in the late 1930s), is *Psalm 67*. Ives wrote an a cappella, bitonal setting, with the female voices in the orbit of C major, the male in that of G minor. He called it 'a kind of enlarged plain chant',[1] and it does remind one of choral psalm settings of the Renaissance, based on a Gregorian psalm tone, in block-chord *falsobordone* style (Ex. 18)—at least in the opening and closing sections, which surround a contrasting fugato in skipping rhythms that is slightly reminiscent, in its sturdy straightforwardness, of the 'fuging tune' style of eighteenth-century New England composers like William Billings.

Ex.18

Andante maestoso

God be mer – ci – ful un – to us, and bless us

© Copyright 1939 by Associated Music Publishers, Inc. Used by permission.

Psalm 150 is shaped like *Psalm 67* in three sections, with the second a fugato. The scoring is for boys' chorus and mixed chorus, with optional organ. Ives exploits the planar possibilities of the two-choir texture by giving the boys frequent long-held chords against which the mixed choir moves in piquant, sometimes grinding, chromatic sideslips (Ex. 19a). The fugal entries of the central section are planned unusually: two cycles of them occur, each proceeding from bass up through soprano, first on G, A, B, and C successively (Ex. 19b), then on A, B, C, and D. Perhaps Ives had in mind the 'Omnes generationes' movement of Bach's *Magnificat*, with its similar procession of fugal entries by rising seconds.

Psalm 54 is also set in A B A' form, with a double canon as the central section. The outer sections are based on whole-tone materials. Sopranos and altos are paired; they are played off against a

[1] *Memos* 178. The subtlety of Ives's ear, and the independent conclusions he drew from it, are well brought out in his comments on the work's initial sonority: 'Harmonically [it] could be (would be in harmony books of nice professors) catalogued as an inversion of the 9th. But . . . it seems to me to be a stronger chord than the 9th —which makes one feel that all inversions are not inversions, not always'.

lower plane of paired tenors and basses. In Verse I (Ex. 20) the tenor-bass complex, singing in augmented triads, marches slowly by whole-tones in lock-step down an octave (from C), rises a semitone, then marches back up again (from C♯) in whole-tones. The

Ex.19

soprano-alto complex, dueting similarly in lock-step, and basically in major thirds (i.e. two whole-tones), weaves rhythmic arabesques around the evenly paced lower voices. Ives brings back this first-section music for the last verses, but he reverses the roles of the two groups (and of course the registers of their two musics). Thus, just as the initial tenor/bass slow march reverses itself—the effect is circular, spatial—so does the entire work. The technique anticipates some practices of Webern, much later.

Ex. 20

Psalm 24 takes a new tack. Its basic idea is that of a double wedge, opening out then closing again. Each verse begins with the chorus (a cappella) on a unison C as central axis; then the voices fan out, wedge-like, from this axis (sopranos rising, basses falling). The interval chosen for this expansion process itself expands from verse to verse, like an opening wedge: the setting of Verse 1 fans out by semitones (Ex. 21), that of Verse 2 by whole-tones, that of

Ex. 21

31

Verse 3 by minor thirds, and so on. After the setting of Verse 7 (expansion by perfect fifths) the process is reversed, though more freely: the structural intervals progressively diminish in size, the outer voices reverse their direction (sopranos now in descending motion, basses ascending), and the shape of the entire work as a double wedge is completed by a return to C.

The discussion above has said little of the text-music relationships or the expressive qualities of these psalm settings. All four works are powerful, to be sure, but they were after all the products of a 19-year-old fledgling, trying his wings in unconventional modes of harmonic, textural, and rhythmic expression. They may well be viewed as 'compositional études', with analogies to the later studies by Milhaud in superimposed chords and bitonality or by Bartók in scales and intervals.

Related in manner to these psalm settings but not so uncompromisingly rigorous in construction is the *Processional: Let There be Light* (1901). Like the 'refrain' sections of *On the Antipodes*, the work is based on chains of ever-different, 'artificially' constructed * chords, all anchored to a constant C in the bass. The second choral phrase (Ex. 22) exemplifies the technique involved; the first is freer harmonically, and other details in the piece suggest that Ives had assimilated into his general vocabulary materials and procedures that earlier had been the stuff of 'études'. The music has considerable expressive value in relation to the text; nevertheless, it has its own abstract inner logic as well, as Ives recognized when he listed the work as performable by trombones (instead of chorus), strings, and organ (see the scorings shown in Ex. 22).

Ives seems to have composed part of the 90th Psalm in 1894, then reworked it to completion and performed it at Central Presbyterian Church. But score and parts were thrown out when the church moved; only in 1923 did he set about reconstructing it, and, as the remaining sketches make clear, he virtually recomposed it. Thus *Psalm 90* as we have it is one of Ives's last works (1923–4); his wife remembered his saying it was the only one that satisfied him.[2] The superb text is lengthy, and Ives's setting, for mixed chorus, organ, bells, and low gong, reflects vividly the expressive contrasts between and even within the verses. It is extremely sectional, but a

---

[2] 'Editors' Notes' to Ives, *Psalm 90*, ed. John Kirkpatrick and Gregg Smith (Bryn Mawr, 1970), p. 3.

number of things keep it from falling apart: it is underscored throughout by an organ-pedal C; the music for each verse is suffused with the colour of one or another of four harmonic idioms

Ex.22

summarized by the organ in an introduction; and the serene diatonicism of the first verse returns for Verses 14–17, surrounded by a nimbus of bells and gong ('as church bells, in the distance'), itself forecast in the introduction. Ives's setting of individual verses is governed by his characterization of each of the introductory harmonic idioms (as shown in the captions of Ex. 23); these harmonies,

Ex.23

however, are not mechanically applied but merely allowed to tint the various verse settings, as for example in Verse 11 (Ex. 24): the harmonic structure associated with 'God's wrath', appearing four times, serves to underline in a natural way the words 'pow'r', 'anger', 'fear', and 'wrath'. The serene final section finds all tensions resolved. The choral harmony is rooted in American hymnody with its relaxed subdominant emphasis. Seemingly in the distance, a nebulous cloud of faint bell sounds shimmers, all the more

nebulous because each bell circles in its own ostinato rhythmic
cycle (Ex. 25): Bell I's cycle is of ten quavers; Bell II's, nine;

Ex.24

Bell III's, twelve; Bell IV's, eight. (Only the last, with the organ,
synchronizes with the regular $\frac{4}{4}$ metre and phrasing of the chorus.)

Religious in impulse and expression if not intended for service
use (Ives once described the work as 'from a "Harvest Festival"')
is the set of three *Harvest Home Chorales* (?1898–?1901) for mixed
chorus, organ, trumpets, and trombones on mid-nineteenth-
century hymn texts (but without musical quotations). Soberly jubilant in their choral expression but with the brass often building to

35

a tumult of pealing praise, they are, wrote Ives, 'a kind of outdoor music and have something in common with the trees, rocks, and

Ex 25

men of the mountains in days before machinery'.[3] What they seem to have in common with these things is a great elemental strength and a tangled yet harmonious co-existence of disparate elements. 'Lord of the Harvest', the second piece of the set, exemplifies these

[3] Letter to Lehman Engel, in *Letters of Composers*, ed. G. Norman and M. L. Shrifte (New York, 1946), pp. 345-6.

qualities most clearly. It is based on three metric planes; in Ives's notation, which forces all three into a $\frac{2}{2}$ metre, their relationship (as 6:9:4) is shown in the diagram below:

Like the deep C of *Processional* or *Psalm 90*, a low C♯ anchors the movement tonally; it sounds throughout. Above it, a twelve-bar cycle of harmonies revolves slowly four and one-half times: (1) alone, as introduction; (2) under a tenor melody; (3) with bass counterpoint added to tenor melody; (4) with soprano/alto duet added to the male-voice pair. There is a pause for two hushed echoes of the end of the phrase 'New praises from our lips shall sound' (chanted freely by the chorus, as a canticle); then finally a truncated repetition of (4), with climactic new instrumental voices, closes the movement. The harmonic cycle on which this cumulative set of variations is based is itself circular: as seen in the introduction (Ex. 26), bars 8–13 are a retrograde of bars 1–6, not note-for-note but bar-for-bar (bar 13 = bar 1, 12 = 2, 11 = 3, etc.). The

Ex. 26

entire movement's structure, elemental and audible, is like a cosmos in which planets orbit around a star, moons around planets, and planets and moons themselves revolve. It has an awesome sense of inexorability, intensified by the slightly faster tempo at which each revolution of the cycle is to be taken. The ending (Ex. 27) is shattering; its F versus C♯ final chord, so inconclusive out of context, is prepared and justified by the double tonal implication, C♯ shifting to F, of the 'prime' choral melody of the tenors (q.v. in Ex. 27).

Ex. 27

At the opposite pole from *Harvest Home Chorales* is the concert cantata *The Celestial Country* (1898–9), for soloists, chorus, organ, and orchestra. For one unused to Ives's stylistic pluralism, it would be difficult to imagine these two contemporaneous works as products of the same composer. In seven movements plus several brief instrumental interludes and an 'intermezzo' for string quartet, the cantata is thoroughly conservative, along the lines of those works by Elgar (*The Dream of Gerontius*) and Parker (*Hora Novissima*)— and, ultimately, Brahms and Mendelssohn—that exemplify the Victorian choral cantata/oratorio. The text, a hymn by Henry Alford, is extravagantly hortatory ('Forward, forward into light!' is its theme), and Ives matches it with long, urgent arcs of melody and rich, energy-laden Romantic harmony. The big work hangs together well, partly because of thematic interconnections between movements (1 and 7; 3, 4, and 6) and partly because of the recurrent 'octad' harmonies—eight-note chords built up by thirds, the only unconventional feature of the work—common to all five of the interludes (see below, p. 43). *The Celestial Country* was performed at Central Presbyterian Church in 1902 and was reviewed favourably (the last time for many years that music by Ives was so received); nevertheless, it was not the kind of music that Ives really wanted to write, and he turned his back on both the choral cantata genre and its conventional style.

The secular choral music by Ives that is extant is scanty; a number of scores are lost or incomplete, and others he left unfinished. Of a baker's dozen of partsongs dating from his preparatory school and university years, less than a handful are complete. These reflect the popularity in American schools of Ives's time of student choral groups, especially male glee clubs. Three Yale songs are pleasant trifles: *A Song of Mory's* (1896), *The Bells of Yale* (1897–8), and *The Boys in Blue* (1897 or later). The disruptive dissonant chords labeled 'cloud sounds' by Ives that appear three times in the manuscript of *The Boys in Blue* may have been ideas toward another work (Ex. 28).

Ex.28

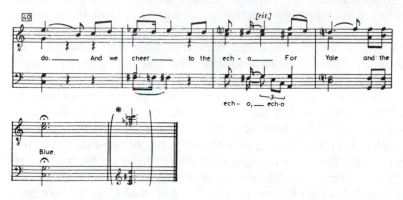

About ten other secular works have in common a scoring for unison chorus (with occasional *divisi*) and varied instrumental ensembles. A number of these were adapted from voiceless ensemble pieces with a principal part for a single instrument under which a text is sometimes to be found—songs 'with or without voices'. In turn, a number were readapted as solo songs for the book of *114 Songs*, such as *Serenity* (originally sketched with an accompaniment for harps and violins), *The New River* (initially a movement in the chamber-orchestra *Set No. 1*, assembled in 1906), *Lincoln the Great Commoner* (with large orchestra), *Majority* or *The Masses*, *He Is There!* (a 'war song march', readapted in 1942 as *They Are There!*), and *An Election*. In these songs for unison chorus and instruments, Ives may have had in mind a Lincolnian 'people's chorus', a mass of voices speaking out as one: almost all are on social or political issues—even, in *The New River* (titled *The Ruined River* in one manuscript), on environmental pollution—and the massed voices, occasionally splitting into heterophonic clusters, have the effect of collective, not individual, statement, as in the passage of *Lincoln the Great Commoner* given as Ex. 29. Of such songs Ives wrote characteristically: 'Probably the old ladies (male

Ex.29

and female) would not—but there are some men who would[—]like to hear some of the choruses with orchestra today[,] especially those about the world problems of the people, etc.[,] sounding up over the stone walls, and "west mountain".'[4]

[4] Ibid.

3. THE KEYBOARD MUSIC

I ves was himself a keyboard player, a professional organist for a number of years and a remarkable pianist, although a private one. John Kirkpatrick, for whom he once played, recalled: 'It was a very flitting kind of playing. He was all over the keyboard. . . . It was a very deft playing [out of] a very contrapuntal mind . . . not limited to the scope of ten fingers.'[1] Of some forty keyboard works by Ives that survive intact, the mature ones, at least, reflect these aspects of his playing: most have a 'flitting' quality, one of mercuriality and quasi-improvisation; in most, the texture is apt to be challengingly contrapuntal; and none is easy to play.

As a keyboard composer, Ives began, as an American boy in the post-Civil-War period might be expected to have begun, with piano marches and sets of variations on well-known hymns and popular and patriotic tunes. Six of the seven extant youthful piano marches he later arranged as band or orchestra pieces, or as songs (e.g. *A Son of a Gambolier* and *The Circus Band*). His earliest variations, on *Jerusalem the Golden* (?1888), are lost, but the second set (?1891), for organ and on *America* (= *God Save the King*), survives —remarkably competent, for a 17-year-old, as well as delectably brash, virtuosic, and funny. The familiar air is foreshadowed in an 'impressive' introduction. After the Theme, in F major, there follow five variations, each of a different character, including a jig-
* ging D♮ transformation, a jogging polonaise version punctuated by giggles in four-foot stops, and a finale beginning 'as fast as the pedals can go' and eventually bringing back the introductory material. The shifts in key between Variations II and III (F to D♭) and IV and V (F minor to F major) are made with a boy's directness (but only an unusual boy's inventiveness): in interludes between

---

[1] Remarks made during a panel discussion in the Charles Ives Centennial Festival-Conference, 17–21 October 1974. Ives can be heard as pianist in re-pressings of some rare private transcriptions in *Charles Ives: The Hundredth Anniversary* (Columbia M4-32504).

the two pairs of variations, the key to come is simply laid over the one being left, in a startling early use of bitonality, and an amusing one (Ex. 30). The piece has other foreshadowings of the mature

Ex.30

Ives, especially in matters of rhythm, such as the twists of phrase-length in Ex. 30 (the F major stratum being foreshortened, the D♭ one elongated) and the cross-rhythms of bars 182–5:[2]

From the same period as the 'America' Variations come four minuscule organ interludes to be played between stanzas of hymns sung by a church congregation. Ives described their style precisely (although he was referring to The Celestial Country): 'I played a short organ Prelude, with eight notes (C E G B♭, D♭ F A♭ C♭) pp in swell organ, pedal playing the main theme f under these' (Memos 33). And he related these piled-up harmonies to a boy's playful imagination: 'This boy's way—of feeling, if you can have two 3rds, major or minor, in a chord, why can't you have another

[2] Pointed out by Ives in Memos, p. 38, where he also mentions another variation that has not survived; it had 'the theme in canon, put in three keys together, B♭–E♭–A♭, and backwards A♭–E♭–B♭ (but this was not played in church concerts, as it made the boys laugh and [be] noisy)'.

43

one or two on top of it[?] it's an obvious and natural way of having a little fun!' (*Memos* 120–1).

A similar spirit ('Why not try it?') may have led to '*Adeste Fidelis*' [sic] *in an Organ Prelude* (1897). What was tried (and it worked) was, first, an inversion of the old hymn tune, then the inversion together with the original melody. Using the same starting-point for both (F), inverting the tune produces a pure Aeolian-mode melody on B♭ (though the melody ends, as it begins, on F), and Ives surrounds the inversion with a soft, sustained B♭ minor triad, 'like distant sounds from a Sabbath horizon', according to a note in the manuscript. In an interlude before the appearance of the original tune (*cum* inversion), and again in an epilogue, this remote chord drifts down chromatically into the orbit of F major; thus the prelude begins and ends in different keys and modes, although in a most natural and unforced way.

In the *Three-Page Sonata* for piano (1905) we confront the rugged, individualistic, 'tough', and mature Ives. The work has satirical aspects: Ives jotted down a memo, to go at its head, which reads 'made mostly as a joke to knock the mollycoddles out of their boxes and to kick out the softy ears!' (*Memos* 155n); the sonata's brevity—announced in its title, which refers to the three manuscript pages the work occupies—is a kind of jab at tradition (of the sort Milhaud was later to perpetrate in his three-minute symphonies and *opéras minutes*); and the manuscript has spoof marginalia like 'Back to 1st Theme—all nice Sonatas must have 1st Theme' and 'repeat 2nd Theme (as is right! and correct)'. Nevertheless, although there are passages of great good humour, the music is seldom funny, and it has depths of inventiveness and integrity that belie its brevity. It may be an anti-sonata, but it is not a parody.

The work is designed in three movements (not indicated as such) defined by tempo changes: Allegro Moderato; Adagio, preceded by an Andante and followed by an echo of it; and Allegro-March Time/Più Mosso, which get a varied repetition before a coda derived from the Allegro-March, so that the movement has the form A B A′ B Coda (A″). The Allegro Moderato is based on the B–A–C–H motive (falling semitone, rising minor third, falling semitone), which permeates the texture in all kinds of guises, disguises, inversions, and permutations. The Adagio is based on bell sounds: Ives invites a second pianist 'or bells-celesta' to perform the chime-like topmost part, and the accompaniment is a combination of middle-register chords, their roots unfocused (like a bell's unusual harmonics), and tolling bass arpeggios on fundamental fifths and tenths. The upper bell-melody almost becomes the tune of Big Ben (*Westminster Chimes*) but never quite achieves it; at its close, like a gramophone record winding down, it crumples limply to rest. Only at the end of the movement, when the preliminary Andante is briefly re-evoked, do we realize that it too is related to *Westminster Chimes*. Despite aspects of vagueness in harmony and melody, the movement has a strong, clear tonal design by virtue of a bass progression that is wholly logical if unique: it gradually descends from g down two octaves to G_1, first in whole-tones, then in chromatic sequences related to B–A–C–H (Ex. 31).

Ex.31

The accompaniment to the bell-melody of the Adagio is worth a close look. Its effect is of a rhythmically vague, improvisatory pair of ostinatos, one a middle-register oscillation of two chords (of a sort to which Schoenberg was exceptionally partial during the period of *Erwartung*), the other a three-note bass arpeggiation that is never quite synchronized with either these chords or the bell-melody. Analysis of the arpeggios reveals that they revolve in rhythmic cycles of five quavers and that Ives systematically exhausts all the possible combinations of two-plus-one quavers (2 + 1 + 2, 1 + 2 + 2, 2 + 2 + 1) or three-plus-one (1 + 1 +3, 3 + 1 + 1, 1 + 3 + 1) that can make up such a cycle of five (Ex. 32).

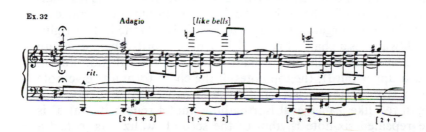

Ex. 32

45

The Allegro-March Time/Più Mosso movement comes closest of the three to being a joke, but an extremely subtle and complex one. The 'March Time' is march-like only to a point; then, over its $\frac{4}{4}$-metre 'oom-pah' bass is laid a waltz rhythm and soon the marching bass is abandoned and a different waltz rhythm takes its place (Ex. 33).

This polyrhythmic and polymetric byplay is intensified in the Più Mosso section, which finds hectic right-hand ragtime rhythms in duple metre competing against a bass also derived from piano-rag style but, contradictorily, in triple metre. All these dance rhythms—march, waltzes, ragtime—are basically simple, jaunty ones, but in context here everything is askew. Obviously, Ives planned very carefully that it be askew, and it should not surprise us that the pitch organization is also carefully planned. The right-hand 'waltz' is a chain of parallel four-note chords (their structure like that of the oscillating ostinato chords in the Adagio, plus an added upper third); the top notes of the chain form a twelve-note series (Ex. 33). The left-hand 'waltz', expressed in octaves, is organized like a medieval isorhythmic motet tenor: its 'talea' is the repeated six-note rhythm of the second 'waltz', its 'color' a

repeating pitch-pattern which falls one note short of being another twelve-note series (Ex. 34). As in many early motets, *talea* and *color* repetitions do not coincide, and thus the more or less rigorous

Ex.34

organization is hidden. The whole passage, in fact, wittily defies the 'mollycoddles' and 'softy ears' to make any sense of it at all. (Ives has them in mind, however, with the last sound of the sonata, a 'nice' C major triad.)

Ives knew neither Schoenberg's music nor medieval motets (at least, not in 1905). Thus the *Three-Page Sonata* exemplifies well his extraordinarily wide-ranging musical mind, which arrived independently at some techniques of musical organization long forgotten (isorhythmic motet technique) and others not yet envisioned (dodecaphony).

Ives's practice of trying out new compositional ideas concretely, in actual works, led him to write a series of short piano pieces which he called 'studies'. Only a few of these remain in complete form. Number 9, *The Anti-Abolitionist Riots in the 1830's and 1840's* (1908), explores multi-level planar heterophony and massive tone clusters (as many as seven notes per hand). Number 21 is *Some Southpaw Pitching!* (?1909). The title uses the American baseball slang for a pitcher who is left-handed, and the piece emphasizes virtuoso left-hand passagework and independence from the right hand's music. The latter derives largely from the melodies of Stephen Foster's *Massa's in de Cold Ground* and the hymn *Antioch* ('Joy to the world')—one team murdered, the other jubilant?—which are closely related musically. Study No. 22 (?1909) concentrates on linear counterpoint, mirrored inversions in close canon, and layered texture with each layer at a different dynamic level.

Related to the *Three-Page Sonata* in its satirical thrust and to the piano studies in being, as subtitled, a 'study . . . for ears or aural and mental exercise!!!' is the late piano work *Varied Air and Variations* (?1923), first published incompletely as *Three Protests*. This is a set of five variations, with other material in the interstices between them, on a theme in octaves that is indeed 'varied': ultra-chromatic, quasi-serially organized, in changing metres, and with virtually no repeated note-durations; Ives characterized it as 'the old stone wall around the orchard', a musical embodiment of the New England stone fence, with none of the stones of exactly the same size or shape. Verbal notes provide a scenario involving a recital. As an introduction, a whimpering protest from the 'box belles' greets 'a man' when he comes onstage to perform; it is heard again after both the bold theme and Variation 1. Variation 2, a march mirrored precisely (and dissonantly) by its inversion, evokes a different moan of protest, which also follows Variation 3, a close, crunching canon. For Variation 4, the 'man' decides, 'All right, Ladies (m[ale] & f[emale]), I'll play the rock line again and harmonize it nice and proper . . . 16 measures, E minor just as much as possible!' This is greeted not by protest but by applause (C major chords, *ffffffffff*). The 'man' reverts to type in Variation 5, furiously combining elements of Variations 2, 1, and 3; and

48

so do the 'ladies', whimpering the first protest for a final time.[3]

The real protests in this composition are of course those of Ives himself—against what he saw as a common confusion of beauty in music with 'something that lets the ears lie back in an easy chair'; against the musical mollycoddles of the concert world; and against, ultimately, the universal rejection and neglect of his music. He went right ahead, however, with his inspired tinkering: contemporaneous with *Varied Air and Variations* were *Three Quarter-tone Pieces* (1923–4) for two pianos, one tuned a quarter-tone sharp. Ives diffidently thought of the Largo and Allegro movements as 'but studies in melodic and rhythmic quarter-tone possibilities', and 'Chorale' (arranged from a string piece, now lost, of 1913–14) as 'little beside a study in quarter-tone harmony' (*Memos* 110–11). The basic idiom of the Largo is that of a number of Ives's gently lyrical, reflective pieces, such as the songs *Evening* and *Afterglow*, enriched by the vibrant shimmer of quarter-tone chordal backgrounds. In the Allegro, which is based on materials from earlier ragtime pieces for theatre orchestra, rapid alternation of the keyboards creates a sizzling, twanging music evocative of a crazy banjo. 'Chorale' borrows melodic motifs from *America* and *La Marseillaise*; the very end of the movement (Ex. 35) shows them in combination (right hand of Piano II) and also shows the 'primary' and 'secondary' quarter-tone chords (marked 'x' and 'y' in Ex. 35) which Ives employs systematically in 'Chorale'. These he constructs ingeniously by interlocking perfect fifths and fourths to build symmetrical quarter-tone complexes; the 'primary' chord has the interval-content of $7 + 7 + 7$ quarter-tones, the 'secondary' chord $5 + 5 + 5 + 5$.[4]

Two giant piano sonatas are the apogee of Ives's keyboard music. The First Sonata is a thirty-minute work in five movements; the Second ('Concord, Mass., 1840–1860'), even longer, is in four. Both are fiercely difficult to perform: although Ives had the 'Concord' Sonata (1910–15) printed privately in 1920—along with the lengthy accompanying *Essays Before a Sonata*—and distributed copies to many musicians, not until 1939 was it publicly played in its entirety (by John Kirkpatrick); the First Sonata (1901–9) waited until 1949 for its first complete performance (by William Masselos).

[3] It would have been characteristic of Ives to keep secret a possible punning version of the title of this work: *Very Darin' Variations*.

[4] Ives discusses these kinds of chords and other aspects of his thinking about quarter-tone music in 'Some "Quarter-tone" Impressions' (1925), reprinted in *Essays*.

'Concord' is programmatic, although in a general way only: Ives said of one movement, 'Not something that happens, but the way something happens' (*Essays* 42). Its movements are titled 'Emerson', 'Hawthorne', 'The Alcotts', and 'Thoreau', and Ives

Ex. 35

✱ Piano I is tuned one quarter-tone higher than Piano II

noted in the preface to his *Essays* that it is 'a group of four pieces, called sonata for want of a more exact name, [that] is an attempt to present (one person's) impression of the spirit of transcendentalism that is associated in the minds of many with Concord, Mass., of over a half century ago.' The First Sonata has no movement titles (except for the second half of one, 'In the Inn', probably because it had had that title in an earlier chamber version), but Ives had in mind a general scenario for the work: 'the family together in the first and last movements, the boy sowing oats in the ragtimes [movements 2 and 4], and the parental anxiety in the middle movement' (*Memos* 75n). Thus, unlike the piano studies, the choral études, or the 'experimental' songs, but like some others of his biggest works (e.g. the Second String Quartet and the Fourth Symphony), the piano sonatas developed as Ives's musical reactions to some of the most profound and complex experiences in his life—to his philosophical background as exemplified in the authors he most admired, and to human relationships, particularly those involving family. This perhaps accounts in large part for the sonatas' being difficult to perform (not only technically) and difficult to follow conceptually (though not viscerally), let alone analyse: they have the flow and flux of musing about big matters, almost in free association; they are not cast in any preconceived moulds, nor are they realizations of pre-compositional plans. Ives himself, in some remarks about 'Concord', characterized the sense of organic growth that pervades them: 'Some of the passages now played haven't been written out . . . and I don't know as I shall ever write them out, as it may take away the daily pleasure of playing this music and seeing it grow and feeling that it is not finished. (I may always have the pleasure of not finishing it)' (*Memos* 79–80). And yet what *is* written out, in each work, makes up a coherent, compelling cycle that deserves no 'more exact name' than 'sonata'.

One key to the coherence of the five movements of the First Sonata is the simple, strong architecture of the whole work: rhapsodic first movement balanced by heroic finale, complementary ragtime scherzos in movements 2 and 4, and a central movement itself quite symmetrical (Largo, Allegro, Largo). Another key is the thematic interconnections between movements. First, third, and fifth movements work with the hymn tune *Lebanon* ('I was a wandering sheep'), second and fourth movements with the three hymn tunes *Happy Day*, *Bringing in the Sheaves*, and *I Hear Thy Welcome Voice* (which are themselves inter-related); and a descending three-note motif—semitone, minor third—increasingly informs the whole work (being heard in the ragtime movements as a jazzily ambiguous third, now major, now minor, over the tonic) until it saturates the texture of the finale. The third movement may be heard as a rhapsodic series of developments of material from *Erie* or *Converse* ('What a friend we have in Jesus'), but it goes beyond that, in a cunning revelation of the relationship between the hymn tune's first phrase and that of Foster's *Massa's in de Cold Ground*.

Hymn tunes, ragtime, Foster melodies—these may seem unpromising raw materials for a work of such power and scope. But as Ives uses them, not as mere dashes of local colour or programmatic indicators, they are audible expressions of his transcendentalist conviction that 'all occupations of man's body and soul in their diversity come from but one mind and soul!' (*Essays* 96). This sense of the oneness of human experience, of the immanence of an Emersonian oversoul in all things, everyday and common-place as well as highly artful, is accomplished concretely by Ives through his choice of musical materials, his perception of inter-relatedness among them, and his fusion of them into a new and convincing synthesis. A single example will here have to suffice, though it cannot begin to suggest the long spans over which Ives throws his net of inter-relationships. The two scherzos are both subdivided. All four sub-movements are of course obviously inter-related by being suffused with ragtime rhythms; movements 2a, 2b ('In the Inn'), and 4b were in fact adapted from an earlier chamber set of *Ragtime Pieces* (1902–4), while 4a—rhythmically the most complicated—was freshly composed for the piano sonata. All are further inter-related by similar conclusions (indicated as 'Chorus' in 2a and 2b), the common thematic source of which is most obviously the refrain of the hymn tune *I Hear Thy Welcome Voice* (Ex. 36a). Less obvious is another source, the 'chorus' of *Massa's in de Cold Ground* (Ex. 36b), although once heard in movement 3

Ex.36
(a) Chorus   I Hear Thy Welcome Voice

Ex.36
(b)   Massa's in de Cold Ground

('Down in the corn-field')

as one of *its* thematic sources—even if there the song's verse, not its 'chorus', is borrowed—the connection is clearer. Example 37 shows the 'Chorus' of movement 2b and its basis in these vernacu-lar source materials—hymn tune/Foster song for the melody and harmony, rag-like syncopation for the inner parts—and their sublimation in a clause of considerable grandeur.

The 'Concord' Sonata has a design as strong and clear as that of the First Sonata, and one closer to traditional sonata structure. 'Emerson' is the weightiest of the movements, powerful and virtually orchestral in texture; it originated as a concerto or overture with piano. 'Hawthorne' is a scherzo that, except at two moments,

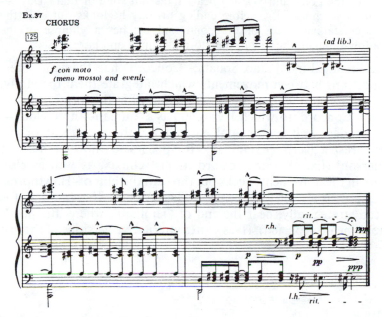

Ex.37

Used by permission (see page 98).

rushes by in a blur; John Kirkpatrick describes it as seeming to be 'pure fantasy, the images following as if helter-skelter but actually in a symmetrical design: phantasmagoria – nocturne – ragtime – contrasts – ragtime – nocturne – phantasmagoria'.[5] 'The Alcotts' functions as the relaxed slow movement of the cycle, a gentle, slightly blurred tintype portrait. 'Thoreau', on the other hand, has no precedent in previous sonatas. Outwardly calm, inwardly intense, its magic is translated verbally by Ives in the only explicit 'programme note' of the *Essays* (67–9):

And if there shall be a program . . . let it follow his thought on an autumn day of Indian summer at Walden—a shadow of a thought at first, colored by the mist and haze over the pond. . . . As the mists rise, there comes a clearer thought more traditional than the first—a meditation more calm. . . . He seems to move with the slow, almost monotonous swaying beat of this autumnal day. . . . His meditations are

[5] Preface to Ives, *Symphony No. 4* (New York, 1965), p. viii.

interrupted only by the faint sound of the Concord bell—'tis prayer-meeting night in the village. . . . It is darker—the poet's flute is heard out over the pond and Walden hears the swan song of that "Day"—and faintly echoes. . . . Before ending his day he looks out over the clear, crystalline water of the pond and catches a glimpse of the "shadow-thought" he saw in the morning's mist and haze. . . .

As in the First Piano Sonata, 'Concord' has thematic inter-connections between movements which integrate them forcefully. Comparable to the three-note abstract motif in the former work is one in 'Concord' to which Ives refers as a 'human-faith melody—transcendent and sentimental enough for the enthusiast or the cynic, respectively' (*Essays* 47). It appears at the first hush in 'Emerson' (Ex. 38a) and toward its last climax, as well as else-where in the movement; peeks out through the blur of 'Hawthorne' (Ex. 38b); is a principal theme of 'The Alcotts' (Ex. 38c); and is placed strategically, near the end of 'Thoreau', where 'the poet's flute' is heard (Ex. 38d). (Ives writes alternative versions of the last

Ex.38
(c)

Moderately

(d)

(For Piano alone)

passage, with flute and without.) This melody often precedes the appearance of another one, universally recognized: the opening motif of Beethoven's Fifth Symphony (see Ex. 38c). But that motif is also important in the hymn tune *Missionary Chant* ('Ye Christian heralds') (Ex. 39a). That Ives was aware of the double association is suggested by his characterization of the motif as 'the soul of humanity knocking at the door of the divine mysteries' (*Essays* 36), and he often lends something of himself to it—gives it a third dimension—by leading it on into a phrase of his own (as at the end of Ex. 38c). Yet another hymn tune, *Martyn* ('Jesus, lover of my soul'), shares with the Beethoven/*Missionary Chant* motif its pitch-pattern (Ex. 39b), and Ives makes clear in 'Concord' that he has all three sources in mind by quoting them separately and integrally —the Beethoven simply as a four-note motif without continuation, *Missionary Chant* in virtually its original form (at the opening of

'The Alcotts'), and *Martyn* almost complete and in hymnbook harmonization (emerging softly out of a dramatic climax in the central 'contrasts' section of 'Hawthorne'). Ultimately, one perceives that all the thematic materials of the sonata relate to one

another (the 'human-faith melody' to the Beethoven/*Missionary Chant*/*Martyn* motif by the three-note upbeat with which it begins). Thus does the network of musical inter-relationships and of extra-musical associations broaden, to make for a transcendental unity in the 'Concord' Sonata.

4. THE CHAMBER MUSIC

IVES wrote comparatively little chamber music, apart from works for chamber or theatre orchestra (which will be taken up in the following chapter). Some fifteen compositions survive; about the same number are incomplete or lost. The extant complete chamber works include four sonatas for violin and piano, two string quartets, a piano trio, and some other pieces mostly in one movement. Except for the quartets, virtually all of these works include piano (as do the majority of the orchestral compositions); Ives seems to have liked the instrument as a 'binder' of some sort.

Leaving aside the so-called 'Pre-First' Violin Sonata (1899–?1903), the surviving movements of which found their way into the other sonatas (except for one, which Ives translated into the *Largo* for violin, clarinet, and piano), the four violin sonatas form a coherent group, more unified in style and expression than any other similar group of Ives's works. Composed between 1902 and 1916, all are in three movements; each has a finale and at least one other movement based on hymn tunes; and all are direct and accessible in expressive content and without showy display or merely 'idiomatic' writing, unless it be the perpetual-motion, across-the-strings, cross-accented style of country fiddling which Ives introduced into the sonata medium, as in the middle movement of the Second Sonata (Ex. 40).

Ex.40

The developments out of hymn tunes, on which almost every movement of the sonatas is based, are among Ives's most ingenious, warm and imaginative. The Fourth Sonata ('Children's Day at the Camp Meeting'; 1906–?16)—actually the first to be sketched—suggests the freedom and variety with which Ives elaborates on his source material. Its second and third movements proceed, like d'Indy's 'Istar' Variations, from obscure hinting at the source, or florid disguise of it, to a more or less clear disclosing of it in conclusion. A comment by Ives on the last movement of the Third Sonata could be applied equally well to these two in the Fourth, and to other movements among the sonatas; it well describes their formal principle: 'The free fantasia is first. The working-out develops into the themes, rather than from them' (Memos 69n). Thus, in the third movement of the Fourth Sonata, Robert Lowry's hymn tune Beautiful River (Ex. 41) is only vaguely perceptible in the opening bars (Ex. 42a) but clearly and completely presented in the last ones (Ex. 42b). The free arabesque of the second move-

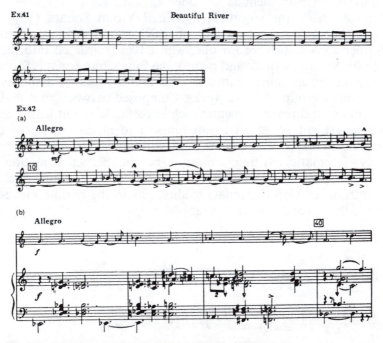

Ex41   Beautiful River

Ex.42
(a) Allegro

(b) Allegro

ment's opening (Ex. 43), largely unbarred, reveals its basis in *Jesus Loves Me!* only with close study: fragments of the opening phrase of the hymn's refrain (Ex. 44) appear—as in B♭, C, and C♯— before the violin enters, in C. (Its underlying G major arpeggios, and the piano's fifth-chord below, provide a logical springboard to full quotation of the hymn bitonally, by fifths, late in the movement.

Ex. 43

Ex. 44

The external design of the violin sonatas is clearly based on the traditional group of movements contrasting in tempo and character, but the design within individual movements is not open to generalization. Except for an occasional A B A′ form, traditional abstract shapes are not to be found; nor are pre-compositional plans of the sort Ives worked out for a number of other compositions. The first movement of the Third Sonata (1913–?14) is related to the scherzos of the First Piano Sonata in that each of four 'verses' (the last three being essentially very free variations on the motives and gestures of material in the first) ends with basically the same 'refrain'. Prototypes of the form are common in American revival hymns, with their several stanzas all ending with a common refrain. In some movements the very experience that inspired the music seems to have suggested its general shape. In the Second Sonata (1907–10), for example, the second movement, which functions as a scherzo, is called 'In the Barn'. The reference is to Saturday nights in the barn, and the music has all the energy, vitality, and non-stop propulsiveness—projecting constantly ahead, never looking back—of a square dance and its chains of 'figures'. The third movement, 'The Revival', opens quietly, ruminatively, almost prayerfully, then like a camp-meeting revival service increases in intensity through a series of mounting dynamic arcs to a frenetic, shouting climax, cathartic and draining at the same time; the music then subsides quickly to a close (how quickly will depend on the performers' feelings), exhausted and purged (Ex. 45).

Ex.45

The two string quartets are as dissimilar stylistically as the violin sonatas are similar. The First Quartet, a youthful product of the Yale years (1896), is in many ways Brahmsian, while the Second Quartet (1907–13), from the period of Ives's most uninhibited and individualistic composition, is thoroughly 'Ivesian'.

Ives subtitled the First Quartet variously as 'A Revival Service' and 'From the Salvation Army'. Its last three movements— 'Prelude', 'Offertory', and 'Postlude'—were composed (for organ?) for church use; the opening 'Chorale' originated as an organ fugue for Parker's class. The fugue is scholastic, down to its $\frac{4}{2}$ metre, inversions, strettos, organ-like pedal points, and final augmentation of the subject. The latter, and one of its countersubjects, must have surprised Parker: they are phrases from Mason's *Missionary Hymn* ('From Greenland's icy mountains') and *Coronation* ('All hail the pow'r of Jesus' name'), by the eighteenth-century American, Oliver Holden. Ives may have chosen the particular phrases because of the relationship, by inversion, of a triad figure common to them (Ex. 46) and because of a chorale-like dignity that they share, stemming partly from their simple, even rhythms. The texture, rhythmic character, and form of the 'Prelude' and 'Postlude' derive from Brahms; less derivative is the 'Offertory', a lyrical elaboration on another hymn tune, *Nettleton* ('Come, thou fount of every blessing').

Ex.46

The Second String Quartet is one of Ives's richest and most original works, on several counts. One is its programmatic conception, and the realization of it in sound. Another is its projection of a kind of musical discourse the implications of which are still being worked through by composers. A third is the musical work as a whole, one of Ives's most subtly integrated, panoramically envisioned, and organically achieved.

The three movements are titled 'Discussion', 'Arguments', and 'The Call of the Mountains'. In a note on the sketches Ives wrote: 'S[tring] Q[uartet] for 4 men—who converse, discuss, argue . . . fight, shake hands, shut up—then walk up the mountain side to view the firmament'. The conversation and discussion, argument and fight, and ultimate joint contemplation are reflected in a moderate-fast-moderate movement plan to which Ives was partial; it fits perfectly the programme of the quartet. So too does the arc of tension, higher tension, and final relaxed sublimity that one can generalize out of the work.

As so often happened with Ives, a specific personal experience led him to compose the quartet: 'After one of those Kneisel Quartet concerts . . . I started a string quartet score, half mad, half in fun, and half to try out, practise, and have some fun with making those men fiddlers get up and do something like men' (*Memos* 74). This led to a radical independence among the four voices of his quartet, sometimes an apparently total unrelatedness among them (each man acting like himself). The result is a 'personalization' of the music to such a degree that it is heard almost anthropomorphically: the first violin is not simply an instrument making musical sounds; it is the embodiment of a human being, as is each of the other instruments. A later composer admittedly influenced by Ives, Elliott Carter, consciously extended this concept of musical discourse (as have other younger composers). Carter has referred to his own works as 'auditory scenarios'; Ives's Second Quartet might also be so characterized.

The approach to a dramatic personification of the four instruments produced a quartet full of extremes of expression and idiom. One hears virtually every kind of melody, harmony, rhythm, phrase structure, plan of dynamics, scoring, and writing for the instruments. (The tendency of the First Quartet to a texture consistently *a 4* is slightly less persistent in the Second.) The wildly varied materials succeed each other abruptly, sometimes violently; sometimes they literally co-exist. Alongside the most radical sort of jagged, wide-spanned, rhythmically disparate, chromatic melody is melody of the simplest stepwise diatonicism. Triadic harmony alternates with fourth- and fifth-chords, chromatic aggregates, and tone clusters. Canons without any harmonic underpinnings follow passages anchored to static harmonic-rhythmic ostinatos. 'Athematic' writing is set side-by-side against passages quoting pre-existent melodies in almost cinematic collage. 'Talea' and 'color' repetitions organized serially (like those analysed in the *Three-Page Sonata*) jostle with diatonic-scale passagework.

These extremes of variety respond to and embody, of course, the notions of 'discussion' and 'arguments', as does the apparently free stream of consciousness with which events unfold, especially in the first two movements. Yet the seemingly unplanned, whimsical, and occasionally downright funny ordering is offset by several controlling factors. One is the C that is the tonal fulcrum of movements 1 and 2 and stabilizes at critical points the otherwise crazy gyrations of harmony and tonality, if only by momentary allusion rather than insistence. Example 47 shows several such points: (a) the beginning of movement 1; (b) the end of its first section; (c) the last of a series of tune quotations, one for each instrument (here it is the cello's turn, paralleled bitonally by violin 1); (d) the end of movement 1; (e) the beginning of movement 2; (f) one of that movement's angry interruptions; and (g) the end of the second

movement, which prepares a cadence on C but abruptly denies it
(the 'arguments' not really being resolved; Ives wrote in the
sketch, 'good place to stop—not end'). Another controlling factor
is the frequent appearance of associative linear techniques like
melodic inversions (see violin 2 and viola in Ex. 47c), intervallic
correspondences (compare the tritone-laden beginnings of movements 1 and 2 in Exx. 47a and 47e), imitations, fugatos, and canons,

Ex.47

(g)

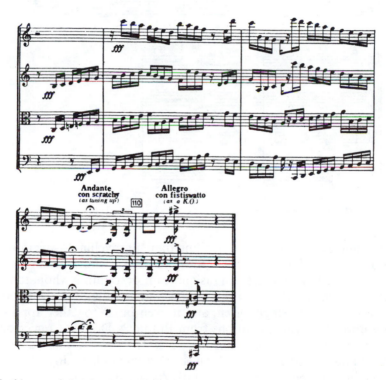

Used by permission (see page 98).

as in the long central section of movement 2 (Ex. 48). The predominance of tritones and minor seconds in the theme shown in Ex. 48 relates back to the first sonority of the work (Ex. 47a), the component intervals of which colour both the harmony and melody in all three movements.

Allegro

Used by permission (see page 98).

Yet another factor, less controlling than 'unravelling'—the most important thread in the fabric of the quartet as a whole—is an idea
*first presented in passing as an insignificant descending whole-tone scale (movement 1, bars 9–10). This idea makes other non-thematic appearances increasingly often, and it even binds together apparently unrelated tune-quotations from Brahms's Double Concerto, *Marching Through Georgia*, *Hail! Columbia* (in the first movement); and *The Star-Spangled Banner* and the 'Ode to Joy' theme of Beethoven's Ninth (in the second). As the third movement begins, the motif has crystallized into a descending three-note figure: we hear it in a fragment of *Nettleton* (bars 9–10) and finally in Mason's *Bethany* (see Ex. 3). *Bethany*, first presented clearly in bars 56ff, in fact turns out to be the goal of the entire quartet: discussion and arguments have given way to joint contemplation of the firmament, and the hymn tune's second strain, interlocked

with *Westminster Chimes* (violin 1), is heard in a splendid epi-phany (Ex. 49). Violin 2 breathes sympathetically below; the viola rocks tranquilly; and the cello strides with relaxed majesty through a descending ostinato (its whole-tone scale bringing the work full circle back to the first hidden appearance of the *Bethany* motif near the opening of the first movement).

Ex. 49

Used by permission (see page 98).

Besides the violin sonatas and the quartets, Ives's chamber music works are mostly rather brief pieces with, however, varying specific gravities. A number are overtly humorous in intent, and some are of the sort Ives described as being 'started as kinds [of] studies, or rather trying out sounds, beats, etc., usually by what is called politely "improvisation on the keyboard"' (*Memos* 61). The longest is a three-movement Trio for violin, cello, and piano (1904–5). Its first movement is an explicit instance of Ives's 'layering' technique: bars 1–27 offer a duet for piano and cello, the cello functioning as the bass; bars 28–52 offer a different duet, for violin and piano; in bars 52–80 the two previous duets are laid one on the other. In retrospect the movement is recalled as a somewhat witty tour de force, for neither duet has seemed lacking in substance and yet the two work well together. The Trio's scherzo is titled 'Tsiaj', which may need explanation, standing for 'This scherzo is a joke'; on one of the sketches, Ives labelled the movement 'Medley on the Campus Fence', referring to the welter of popular, patriotic, and student songs quoted in it in ludicrous profusion.

Related in spirit to the scherzo of the Trio is that of *A Set of 3 Short Pieces* (?1908).[1] Scored for string quartet, it is a brief tripartite piece, plus three final dissonant eight-note chords ('as three cheers'). Deceptively simple and amusing, it is actually full of knotty polyrhythms; in his manuscript sketch Ives referred to the middle section (Ex. 50) as 'practice for String Q't in holding your own!' The kind of 'mensuration canon' technique it embodies is found even earlier in Ives, not in the wilfully playful spirit of the string scherzo but with rather more exalted aims, in *From the Steeples and the Mountains* (1901–?2), for trumpet, trombone, and four sets of eight bells each. This is a music of planes within planes: the brass duo forms one plane, against a backdrop of bells; but each set of bells is treated also as a sub-plane. The brass melodies are angular, asymmetrical, and chromatic, and their relationship is elusive as they keep slipping in and out of canons with each other. Each of the bell melodies begins with scales, then shifts to change-ringing patterns, then to jangling diads, finally to hard-struck triads—all diatonic but in different keys (Bells 1 and 4 in C, Bells 2 in D♭, Bells 3 in B). They are differentiated rhythmically as well: they begin together but soon go out of phase, like a mensuration canon, as each begins a new pattern of even notes at a slightly different moment, in a carefully notated process of gradual acceleration (the patterns are, successively, in notes of the following values: ♩ ♩. ♪ ♪ ♪ ♪ and ♪) and deceleration (by a reverse process).

The dynamic plan of both brasses' and bells' planes is a steady

[1] Ives liked the term 'set' for a group of pieces put together, yet not a dance suite or a symphony or sonata cycle. Perhaps it had a connotation of informality and plainness that appealed to him, and there is a hint that 'symphony', at least, connoted for him a 'nice' conservatism in his remark that 'the *First Orchestral Set* [is] called *Three Places in New England* (though before it had the nice name of *New England Symphony*)' (*Memos* 83). See also his remarks concerning *New England Holidays*, quoted on p. 84 below.

crescendo until the final pealing chords, which are then allowed to fade naturally to extinction. Ives suggested a general programme for the work in a note at the end of the score: 'From the Steeples—the Bells—then the Rocks on the Mountains begin to shout!'

Ex.50

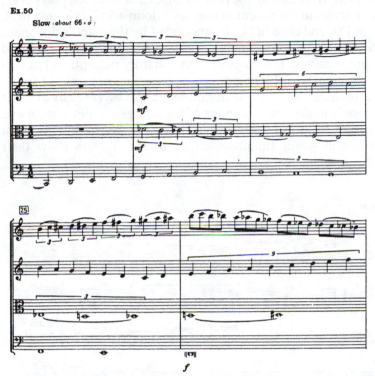

Given adequate sets of bells (the ideal would be church bells sounding from different belfries), the planned tumult and organized confusion of this work is overwhelming; latent in it is the kind of vision that would ultimately lead Ives to plot the 'representation of the eternal pulse & planetary motion of the earth & universe' in his sketches for *Universe Symphony*.

'Organized confusion' well describes yet another chamber work: *Hallowe'en* (1906), for string quartet, piano, and optional drum. In Ives's day (and still, to some degree) Hallowe'en was a night for leaping bonfires, pranks and practical jokes, 'tricks or treats'—a children's-party night. This was the sense that Ives sought to convey in this tiny work (14 bars plus a 4-bar coda). It is to be played several times, each time by a different combination of instruments, each time faster and louder ('keeping up with the bonfire'), until the last go-around, when all players are to join in 'as fast as possible without disabling any player or instrument'. The 'confusion' of the piece is created by the four strings, each of which plays even, rushing scales in a different major key (violin 1 in C, violin 2 in B, viola in D♭, and cello in D), compounded by the piano's dissonant cluster-chords, of increasingly irregular durations, directions, and root-progressions. The 'organization'—hardly perceptible but surprisingly rigorous—Ives described as 'canonic, not only in tones, but in phrases, accents, and durations or spaces' (*Memos* 91). His reference is to the double canons of the strings—violin 1/viola and violin 2/cello—which can better be shown as in Ex. 51 than described in words (numbers added to the phrases show their lengths in semiquavers).

Ex.51

Used by permission of the publishers, Mobart Music Publications, Inc., Hillsdale, N.Y.

70

Written in the same year as *Hallowe'en* are two other brief chamber works that fall into Ives's category of 'kinds of studies . . . trying out sounds, beats, etc.' They are both titled *Largo Risoluto*; No. 1 is a rhythmic study, 'as to the law of diminishing returns', No. 2 a study in simultaneous multiple dynamic levels and what happens when, upon repetition, the dynamics of the various parts are switched around. (At the end of one manuscript score of No. 2 is a suggestive title: 'A Shadow made—A Silhouette'.) Both Largos are scored for string quartet and piano, as is *In re con moto et al* (1913), which Ives described as 'studies in rhythm, time, duration, space, pulse, metre, accent, together and in various ways'. *All the Way Round and Back* (1906), for bugle, clarinet, violin, bells, and piano four-hands, is 'but a trying to take off, in sounds and rhythms, a very common thing in a back lot [baseball game]—a foul ball—and the base runner on 3rd has to go all the way back to 1st' (*Memos* 62).

Baseball games and Hallowe'en parties, described in terms of studies in sounds and rhythms and of canons? Such unlikely conjunctions lead to a conclusion for this chapter, which has alternated constantly between discussion of compositional technique and extra-musical matters, of abstract designs and collage-like tune-quotations, and between objective analysis and subjective description. Such dichotomies are inherent in Ives's music, and also in his thought about it. He made this clear in some remarks about *Hallowe'en*:

The . . . little piece is but a take-off of a Halloween party and bonfire . . . it may not be a good joke, [but] the joke of it is: if it isn't a joke, it isn't anything. [Yet] in spite of the subject matter, this was one of the most carefully worked out (technically speaking), and one of the best pieces (from the standpoint of workmanship) that I've ever done. . . . I happened to get exactly the effect I had in mind, which is the only ([or] at least an important) function of good workmanship. (*Memos* 90–1)

As we have seen, Ives often had very concrete subject matter in mind for a work. One of his major achievements was to bring to bear on that subject matter a highly original musical imagination and to translate it into cogent soundscapes—in part along traditional lines but in larger part not—through 'good workmanship'. The nature of the workmanship is sometimes difficult to perceive—indeed, some have claimed it to be lacking—since both its goals and the materials and musical events being 'worked' are apt to be radically uncommon, some without precedent. As Ives said, 'In picturing the excitement, sounds and songs across the [football] field and grandstand, you could not do it with a nice fugue in C' (*Memos* 40).

5. THE ORCHESTRAL MUSIC

LIKE his songs, Ives's music for orchestra covers the entire span of his composing life. About thirty orchestral works survive in complete form; approximately the same number are incomplete or lost. They are scored for two kinds of ensembles, small and large: theatre or chamber orchestra and full symphony orchestra.

Ives engagingly explained the background of his 'theatre orchestra' ensembles and their motley character:

The make-up of the average theatre orchestra of some years ago, in the towns and smaller cities, in this part of the country, was neither arbitrary nor a matter of machinery. It depended somewhat on what players and instruments happened to be around. Its size would run from four or five to fifteen or twenty, and the four or five often had to do the job of twenty without getting put out. . . . Its scores were subject to make-shifts, and were often written with that in mind. There were usually one or two treble Wood-Wind, a Trombone, a Cornet, sometimes a Saxophone, Strings, Piano and a Drum—often an octave of High Bells [glockenspiel or 'orchestra bells'] or a Xylophone. The pianist usually led—his head or any unemployed limb acting as a kind of Ictusorgan.[1]

Writing out of this background (which he knew well from boyhood in Danbury and from the times when he was occasional pianist in the Hyperion Theater Orchestra in New Haven and later in New York theatres), Ives first composed 'popular entertainment' pieces: marches like *Holiday Quickstep* (1887) and the hilariously parodistic *'Country Band' March* (1903)—an American equivalent of Mozart's *Musical Joke*—or ragtimes like the group of four *Ragtime Pieces* (1902–4). He made a sole venture into incidental music with *Overture and March: '1776'*, composed in 1903 for a play that was never produced. Later, in the decade between 1906 and 1916, there developed out of the theatre-orchestra background some of his

---

[1] Notes by the composer in the original New Music edition of the *Set for Theatre or Chamber Orchestra* (San Francisco, 1932), p. [24].

most extraordinary works. Together, all these compositions cover a huge range of concept, content, and technique; what they have in common is an instrumentation that varies from piece to piece and moreover is apt to be flexible within single pieces. On the one hand Ives seems to have chosen the instrumentation for each work wholly in terms of its expressive aims, as if there were no such thing as a 'standard' chamber-orchestra instrumentation (and in fact there was not). On the other hand he often offers alternate choices of instrumentation for individual parts, suggests omissions of notes if doubling instruments should be insufficient, or cues the notes of one instrument in the part of another should the ensemble lack the complement 'ideally' called for. Such options—so cheerfully offered, so foreign to the music of Ives's contemporaries—remind us of similar ones mentioned earlier: 'ossia' possibilities for either singer or pianist in some songs, alternative scorings in some choral works, the passage in 'Thoreau' to be played either with or without flute added to the pianoforte, repetitions of passages in the violin sonatas to be made at the performers' discretion. Although never a composer of self-conscious 'Gebrauchsmusik' (not even the term had yet been coined), Ives clearly allowed for practical expediency and the exigencies of informal music-making; important to this attitude was his experience of town bands and theatre orchestras and their make-up: ad hoc, not foreordained and immutable; dependent on the players and instruments that 'happened to be around'.

This open-mindedness extends even to the medium of a number of compositions which we may group together as 'songs with or without voices' like those mentioned in Chapter 2: *The Pond*, *The Rainbow*, the *Set for Theatre or Chamber Orchestra*, and several other theatre-orchestra sets in various states of completeness. Some of the individual movements were born as songs for voice and piano, then translated into theatre-orchestra pieces; even more of them went in the opposite direction, from theatre-orchestra pieces to songs. *The Pond* (1906) began life on the fence, so to speak, as an orchestral work for flute (or one violin in harmonics), two harps (with celesta or high bells replacing one if desired), piano, and strings—plus a principal melodic part, with text but marked as for voice or trumpet or basset horn. (Adapted in 1921 for *114 Songs*, it was indexed there by Ives under a different title, *Remembrance*.) Similarly, *The Rainbow* (1914) has a leading cantabile part, with a text, for either basset horn or voice.

Ives clearly viewed the musical work as malleable, to be realized by the performing forces at hand; and he willingly deferred to the performers without insisting on sovereign control. In this kind of attitude, prophetic of the stance of a John Cage, Ives stands at the head of a new view of the relationship between composer and performer, the latter being allowed a considerably greater measure of freedom (or responsibility, to look at it from the other direction) than had been traditional in Western music. One might say that Ives viewed his works not as musical objects but as the stuff of potential experiences to be shaped and realized variously by performers and listeners.

If the compositions just cited exemplify this flexibility in choices of instrumentation and medium, a work like the scherzo *Over the Pavements* (1906–13) exemplifies it in formal aspects as well. Its instrumentation is that of a small theatre orchestra without strings: clarinet, bassoon (or saxophone), trumpet, piano, and percussion; piccolo and three trombones may be added optionally. Its form is sectional and virtually symmetrical: A B C cadenza B′ C′ A′. However, the cadenza at the centre of the piece need not be played: the manuscript reads, 'To play or not to play? If played, to be played as not a nice one—but EVENLY, Precise and unmusical as possible!' *Over the Pavements* had its inception in one of those real-life situations that so frequently led Ives into radical musical transmutations: 'In the early morning, the sounds of people going to and fro, all different steps . . . the horses, fast trot, canter, sometimes slowing up into a walk . . . an occasional trolley throwing all rhythm out' (*Memos* 62). All these different rhythms, beats, time going on together are presented in a score with a staggeringly complex texture; the work is one of Ives's most extreme examples of rhythmic counterpoint. But his initial reaction to the sounds mingling 'over the pavements', one of interested and amused observation, is projected through perky ragtime syncopes and jazzy blue notes, and ultimately an air-clearing, ironic concession to the struggling players—an ending that finds them all together in an oom-pah, oom-pah vamp on a simple C major chord.

Two of the three movements of the *Theatre Orchestra Set* (1906–11) have been cited earlier, but in transformations: 'In the Cage' in its song version and 'In the Inn' in its reincarnation as one of the ragtimes of the First Piano Sonata. (Actually, as mentioned, the set's 'In the Inn' was a second stage itself, derived from one of the *Ragtime Pieces*.) The third movement is 'In the Night', a song without voice (having a solo part with text but, according to the composer's note, one not to be sung). So many alternative instrumentations are offered that it would be tedious to list them— although, wrote Ives in his notes for the published score, 'Whatever the arrangement of players and instruments, the Solo part [for English horn, clarinet, French horn, or trombone, depending on the size of the orchestra] should be clearly heard'. The sinuous, lazy curve of this principal melody (Ex. 52) is notated rhythmically in minute detail, mostly in ♪♫♫♪ and subdivisions thereof. The aim, however, is not one of finicky exactitude but the opposite —a sense of ruminative freedom—and Ives suggests that the 7:6 rhythm (in 3/4 time) need not be observed too literally, so long as the phrases do not coincide with the basic beats.

Ex.52

[Oh! I hear the owl a-hoot-in' in the dark-ness of]

[the night, and it brings the drops of sweat out on my brow]

The melody is projected against a vibrant, palpitating background (Ex. 53a)—a line of warmly luminous colour against a dark wash—in a paradigm of an orchestral texture Ives was particularly fond of. The background 'vibrates' through the interplay of five planes of rhythmic ostinatos and near-ostinatos so planned as hardly ever to coincide, either with each other or with the phrases of the melody. These ostinatos are shown, in greatly simplified abstraction, in Ex. 53b. The harmonic plan of the movement is statically tonal, centered on D♭, but with B♭ chords replacing the dominant (one tone high) and E major chords replacing the subdominant (one tone low), a choice made not arbitrarily but because of the tones of the D♭ triad shared by the other two. These relations are preserved in the principal melody (in E) and two others which sneak in around it and succeed it to the end of the movement —the 'Down in the cornfield' phrase of Foster's *Massa's in de Cold Ground* (B♭, in high bells) and the hymn tune *Eventide* ('Abide with me') (D♭, in solo cello).

Ives's most frequently performed orchestral work, *The Unanswered Question* ('A Cosmic Landscape'), is usually pro-

Ex. 53

grammed as an independent piece, and with a full symphonic complement of strings (plus its solo woodwinds and single trumpet). But it is related to the theatre-orchestra tradition (third and fourth flutes replaceable by oboe and clarinet, the solo trumpet by an English horn, oboe, or clarinet; the woodwinds not to play their notated rhythms strictly but freely, 'in somewhat of an impromptu way'), and it was conceived along with *Central Park in the Dark* as one of a complementary pair of 'contemplations'. Their original titles were: I. 'A Contemplation of a Serious Matter' or 'The Unanswered Perennial Question' and II. 'A Contemplation of Nothing Serious' or 'Central Park in the Dark in the Good Old Summertime'. Both works date from 1906 and, as Ives's titles suggest, are related as opposites. In *The Unanswered Question* a wholly diatonic and mostly triadic wash of strings is background for an atonal, chromatic foreground of winds; in *Central Park* a chromatic, atonal string background is set behind tuneful 'popular' material in solo wind and brass instruments, percussion, and two pianos. The metaphysical programme of *The Unanswered Question* —the strings representing 'the silence of the druids', the trumpet asking 'the perennial question of existence', and the flutes ('Fighting Answerers') attempting to find a satisfactory response—is opposed to *Central Park*'s terrestrial, urban 'picture-in-sounds of . . . happenings that men would hear some thirty or so years ago (before the combustion engine and radio monopolized the earth and air), when sitting on a bench in Central Park on a hot summer night'.[2]

The two works have in common an unprecedented, visionary realization of space and time in music. Each suspends multiple, discrete musics in a delicate balance. In *The Unanswered Question* there are three such musics: the strings' gauzy backdrop of continuous slow-motion pastel harmonies, to be played offstage; the trumpet's disturbingly repetitive atonal interjections, unsynchronized with the strings; and the woodwinds' increasingly accelerated, agitated, and raucous responses to the trumpet (Ex. 54). In *Central Park* there are basically two musics: the background string music, turning slowly in spirals through a ten-bar phrase (Ex. 55) stated ten times, always 'molto adagio', always *ppp*; against this, a cumulative appearance 'onstage' of popular musicians—each entering instrument seeming to try to upstage those already there—in a steady crescendo, accelerando, and growing density to a saturation

[2] Notes by the composer in the published scores of *The Unanswered Question* (New York, 1953), p. 3, and *Central Park in the Dark* (Hillsdale, 1973), p. [31].

78

of the musical space in a shouting climax, after which the strings continue imperturbably: 'again the darkness is heard—an echo over the pond—and we walk home', reads Ives's note in the score.

Used by permission (see page 98).

Both works are famous as precursors of the 'stereophonic' and collage techniques of such composers as Stockhausen, Berio, Cage, Carter, and Brant. But perhaps even more radical than these aspects (which, after all, had been foreshadowed in the collage-like simultaneous dance orchestras of *Don Giovanni* and the spatially determined polychoral works of Giovanni Gabrieli and Orazio Benevoli) is Ives's achievement of a new relationship between time and music. This has to do mainly with the elimination of a sense of beat or pulse—the even 'measuring' of time—that had been common to all Western music for centuries. The string music of *The Unanswered Question* is notated in even $\frac{4}{4}$ bars, but it is so disposed rhythmically that a pulse is imperceptible: it moves very, very slowly; it has no symmetries or predictabilities of phrase shapes; one part's phrases do not coincide with those of any other. In *Central Park* the string music, spiralling in a more dynamic series of curves than those of *The Unanswered Question* (but still very slowly), nevertheless does not 'measure' time, because of the irrational, asymmetrical lengths of the phrases and notes. The ten-bar span is divided into four segments (see the bass part in Ex. 55) but the division is one of an unpredictable 2 + 3 + 3 + 2 bars; the

Ex.55

Used by permission of the publishers, Mobart Music Publications, Inc., Hillsdale, N.Y.

harmonic structure confirms the division (but also the unpredictability) by shifting from augmented triads (bars 1–2) to fourth-chords (bars 3–5) to chords built of alternating augmented fourths and perfect fifths (bars 6–8) to fifth-chords (bars 9–10). Within the large span smaller phrases shape themselves, but no two are of the same length, and *gruppetti* (3:4, 5:4) wash away any pulse. Schoenberg spoke of his 'emancipation of the dissonance'. By analogy, we might say that Ives 'emancipated rhythm' from its ancient ties to

80

metre and pulse. In fact, in the string music of *Two Contemplations* as at times in others of Ives's mature works, 'time' in the usual musical sense does not exist; the only time-sense is of the chronological continuum, and the music simply unrolls in it—like a scroll in space, at once plastic and concrete.

Ives's principal works for large orchestra are four numbered symphonies, the group of four pieces first called *Holidays Symphony*, the *Robert Browning Overture*, two three-movement 'sets' (and a third unfinished), and a sketched but never completed *Universe Symphony*.

Earliest of these are the first three symphonies. The First (completed 1898) is a remarkably competent graduation exercise, written at Yale in a traditional but not old-fashioned manner under Horatio Parker's guidance (and strictures); it shows both an influence and a mastery of Brahms's and Dvořák's symphonic styles. The Second (1900–2) is a more liberated cycle—an accurate term considering the inter-movement thematic links and a coda reworking material from earlier movements together with some from the last. It is 'Americanized' by extensive use of popular, patriotic, and hymn tunes but is uneven and discursive, a kind of symphonic counterpart to *The Celestial Country* and relating to Ives's orchestral works of 1906 and later much as *Verklärte Nacht* relates to the *Five Pieces for Orchestra* and later works of Schoenberg.[3] In the Third Symphony (1904) Ives approached the medium more freshly and independently. The scoring is lighter (single woodwinds, two horns, one trombone, and strings, with bells ad lib. at the very end), the texture leaner and more contrapuntal, the rhythmic shapes more supple and subtle. Derived from earlier chamber pieces made for church use, the symphony is subtitled 'The Camp Meeting' and its themes are largely based on hymn tunes. One of these, *Woodworth* ('Just as I am, without one plea') (Ex. 56), is used in all three movements, not merely 'quoted' but developed integrally (Ex. 57);

[3] The most startling sound in Ives's Second is the magnificent eleven-note squawk of its final chord, but this was a replacement for the original F major tonic chords which was made by Ives in preparing the symphony for publication early in the 1950s. In a review of the first performance (22 February 1951) Henry Cowell reported Ives as saying that such a discordant blast was 'a formula for signifying the very end of the very last dance [of an evening]: the players played any old note, good and loud, for the last chord' (*Musical Quarterly*, xxxvii (1951), pp. 399–402).

along with *Azmon*, similarly elaborated upon, it contributes to the broad hymnic dignity of the outer movements, which flank a livelier middle one titled 'Children's Day'.

Ex.56

Ex.57

(a)

First movement

b

Second movement

(c) Third movement

Between the Third Symphony and the completion of the Fourth, Ives wrote four other works of symphonic dimensions. First was *New England Holidays* (1904–13)—'Holiday Symphony—but not called Sym as 1st theme is not in C and 2nd [not in] G', wrote Ives with characteristic anti-establishment sassiness on one sketch. This is an American 'Four Seasons' as reflected in national holidays: 'Washington's Birthday' (winter), 'Decoration Day' (spring), 'The Fourth of July' (summer), and 'Thanksgiving' (autumn). These are nostalgic pieces 'based on something of the memory that a man has of his boyhood holidays' (*Memos* 95), which partially explains their being filled with bald tune-quotations, not so much developed as coming to mind, some half-recalled or even mis-remembered,[4] singly or in fantastic juxtapositions or superimpositions, as in a barn dance section of 'Washington's Birthday' (Ex. 58) which finds *Turkey in the Straw* (flute) crazily out of step (and key) with *The White Cockade* (violin), or the climax of 'The Fourth of July',

Ex.58

where wildly off-key and off-rhythm versions of *Katy Darling*, *The Battle Hymn of the Republic* (both its verse, 'Mine eyes have seen the glory of the coming of the Lord', and its refrain, 'Glory, glory, Hallelujah!'), *Columbia, the Gem of the Ocean*, and *Yankee Doodle*

---

[4] This is not to imply that none has structural significance. Regarding 'The Fourth of July', for instance, Dennis Marshall has pointed out in a perceptive article on 'Charles Ives's Quotations: Manner or Substance?', *Perspectives of New Music*, vi (1968), pp. 45–56, that *Columbia, the Gem of the Ocean* 'serves as a structural framework for the entire movement in much the same way that a Lutheran chorale melody would serve as the formal model and motivic source for a cantata movement or an organ chorale prelude of J. S. Bach'.

are only part of the festive pandemonium (Ex. 59). 'Decoration Day' projects a remarkable balance between the boisterous joyousness of children at a street parade (with two bands playing different *

Ex. 59

marches simultaneously) and reverence; one sensitive and touching moment in the piece (which for Ives concerned the holiday dedicated to the dead of the Civil War) finds the slow bugle-call *Taps* accompanied by Mason's *Bethany*.

The twenty-minute-long *Robert Browning Overture* (1908–12), the only one of a projected series of orchestral movements on 'Men of Literature' completed by Ives, is scored for a large conventional orchestra but, in the noisy sections, with the strings divided into as many as thirteen parts. It is a work of violent sectional contrasts: a slow, germinating introduction; a ferocious, dense-textured Allegro with a wide-intervalled treble march melody in nine-note parallel chords superimposed on a faster marching bass (their tempos are in the ratio 2:3); a tender, tranquil set of Adagio variations somewhat Mahleresque in character; a literal repeat of the Allegro; and a fast fugal coda leading to a furious finale—which, however, is cut off abruptly, leaving a momentary echo of the Adagio vibrating in the air. The sense of 'toughness' projected in the Allegro arises partly from the higher-pitched march's chromatic scales with frequent octave-displacements (minor ninths or major sevenths replacing semitones) opposing the steady tramp of the lower-pitched, faster march (Ex. 60).

Three Places in New England (1908–?14)—the First Orchestral Set—is in three movements, in Ives's preferred slow-fast-slow movement order, as is the Second Orchestral Set (1909, 1915). The former is more often played, perhaps because it was first published in a small-orchestra revision made by Ives in 1929, perhaps because its three movements are more sharply etched and contrasting than

Ex.60

those of the Second Set. The first movement, inspired by a bas-relief by Augustus Saint-Gaudens celebrating a Negro regiment in the Civil War, is a brooding 'Black March' (as Ives often called it) with extremely subtle interplay between themes out of Foster's *Old Black Joe* and two Civil War songs, George Root's *Battle Cry of Freedom* and Henry Clay Work's *Marching Through Georgia*. As shown in Ex. 61, for instance, Ives finds a common denominator ('w' in the example) between the phrase 'I'm coming' of Foster's song and '[Hur]rah! Hurrah!' in Work's; combines this with the refrain ('The Union forever, Hurrah boys, Hurrah!') of Root's song ('x'); derives an ostinato bass ('y_1') from a motive shared by the two Civil War songs ('y_2'); and underscores the whole complex with a traditional military band's drumbeat ('z'). The second movement, 'Putnam's Camp', is a boy's fantasies as he surveys a Revolutionary War memorial at an old campsite; it combines the gay, brassy music of a Fourth of July picnic (with the mixups and mistakes of the village band in music adapted from '*Country Band*' *March* and '*1776*') and the boy's hallucinatory vision of ghostly military musicians. In the middle section, the march beat of Ex. 61 ('z') goes along at two different speeds in the proportion 𝅝 ∙ = 𝅗𝅥. in a famous instance of Ivesian polytempo. *Three Places* concludes

86

with a riverside revery, 'The Housatonic at Stockbridge', in which
murmuring waters, swelling then ebbing, and mists in the river
valley are evoked in meandering chromatic swirls, with 'cloud
sounds' circling above them, while a gently curving, freely develop-
ing melody spins itself out in the middle of the texture. This

Ex. 61

melody, later adapted to a text by Robert Underwood Johnson for
114 Songs, is a remarkable arabesque, a testament to Ives as
melodist—so free and unforced and inevitable one is hardly aware
of the recurrences in it of the opening phrase of *Missionary Chant*.*

The Second Orchestral Set also begins with a moody slow movement, 'An Elegy to Our Forefathers'. Originally titled 'An Elegy to
Stephen Foster' and worked on at the same time as the 'Black
March' of *Three Places*, it has a similar character. All the sharp
edges of a march are softened, however, by off-beat and off-metre
rhythmic groupings which dissolve both beat and metre, an effect
all the more astonishing since the movement is based on a persistent brief ostinato throughout: D♭ B♭ D♭ (= 'I'm coming', from
Foster's *Old Black Joe*). Fragments of several Foster songs provide
the thematic material; they too are blurred rhythmically and
melodically so that their separate identities melt into one another
in a soft haze. The second movement, 'The Rockstrewn Hills Join
in the People's Outdoor Meeting', is one of Ives's revival-hymn/
ragtime movements, with a crackling piano part that brings it to
the brink of concertodom, and a final 'Chorus' adapted from the

Ragtime Pieces for theatre orchestra (the same one found in the scherzos of the First Piano Sonata).[5]

The last movement of the Second Set is the most boldly conceived of the three, one of Ives's most amazing transliterations into music of the experience of a real-life incident. The title, 'From Hanover Square North, at the End of a Tragic Day, the Voice of the People Again Arose', is not very helpful in understanding what generated the piece and what it is about; Ives's account in his *Memos* (92–3) is more so:

The morning paper on the breakfast table gave the news of the sinking of the Lusitania [7 May 1915]. . . . Leaving the office [that afternoon], I took the Third Avenue "L" [train] at Hanover Square Station. . . . While waiting there, a hand-organ or hurdy-gurdy was playing in the street below. Some workmen sitting on the side of the tracks began to whistle the tune, and others began to sing or hum the refrain . . . and finally it seemed to me that everybody was singing this tune. . . . There was a feeling of dignity through all this. . . . It was (only) the refrain of an old Gospel hymn . . . *In the Sweet Bye and Bye.*

The scoring of the movement is complex: two orchestras are called for, one a 'Distant Choir' of two violins, viola, French horn, harp, piano, chimes, and basses, plus unison voices briefly at the beginning of the movement. Eventually this distant choir is submerged beneath or absorbed into the main orchestra, a normal symphonic ensemble but with accordions, solo piano, organ, and rich percussion group. The gist of the piece is like Ives's description of the incident that sparked it: a long, slow, increasing collaboration of separate individuals (but all of one mind) gathering force and power—not with outward excitement or agitation but inner fervour and dignity—to a radiant, climactic moment of exaltation. Although by this point (Ex. 62, pp. 90–1) the musical texture has become phenomenally rich in independent melodic-rhythmic voices, the thematic materials of the movement have been very few, essentially two: the opening vocal intonation of the Te Deum chanted as a canticle ('We praise Thee, O God; we acknowledge Thee to be the Lord . . .') and the gospel hymn tune *Sweet By-and-By* ('There's a land that is fairer than day'), which eventually takes

[5] For his recording of the Second Set, Leopold Stokowski either misinterpreted the rubric 'Chorus' (= refrain) as calling for voices or simply could not resist adding them (wordlessly) at this grand climax. (Ives might not have disapproved.)

over entirely, having absorbed from the intonation its atmosphere of timelessness and universality (certainly seeming to have done so). The force and richness of the climax subsist not only in the saturated texture and the almost irresistibly evangelistic music of the 'Chorus' of the hymn tune (cf. Trumpet 3 vs. Accordion Chorus in Ex. 62) but in the harmonic saturation as well. There is no mistaking the F major triumph, but it is strongly coloured by D major and F♯ major/minor material as well, in a startling conjunction (for which, however, Ives has prepared from the very opening of the movement). There is perhaps no more spine-tingling moment in Ives's works than this one.

Ives's last two large-orchestra works, the Fourth Symphony and *Universe Symphony*, are in the line of the two piano sonatas, the Second String Quartet, *The Unanswered Question*, and 'From Hanover Square North' in embodying in music thoughts and feelings and convictions about fundamental human issues. Ives's expanding vision of a music that would be 'a part of the great organic flow, onwards and always upwards' (*Memos* 136) and that would develop 'possibilities inconceivable now—a language so transcendent that its heights and depths will be common to all mankind' (*Essays* 8) found its most complete expression in the Fourth Symphony, which occupied him off and on between 1909 and 1916. It might have found even more surpassing expression in *Universe*, at which he worked from 1915 to 1928 (having first imagined it in 1911), but *Universe* never got much beyond the preliminary stages: some forty-four pages of sketches remain; others, perhaps many, are lost.

The Fourth Symphony is Ives's mightiest complete work. It is not so long as *The Celestial Country* or either of the piano sonatas, but it seems longer, partly because of the sheer weight of the performance forces required, partly because of its more complete stylistic synthesis, partly because it is a giant vessel into which the energies, ideas, and gestures of earlier works flowed. (In fact, no fewer than fifteen prior works by Ives lay behind it and contributed specifics to it.) Like virtually every instrumental piece by Ives, it arose out of so-called extra-musical ideas; it has a 'programme'. But the programme is ultra-general and open to different readings, just as the music invites different listenings (not just re-hearings). For a performance of two movements in 1927, notes were written by Ives's friend Henry Bellamann, certainly from information supplied by the composer:

Ex. 62

Used by permission (see page 98).

This symphony . . . consists of four movements,—a prelude, a majestic fugue, a third movement in comedy vein, and a finale of transcendent spiritual content. [The order of the second and third movements was later reversed.] The aesthetic program of the work is . . . the searching questions of What? and Why? which the spirit of man asks of life. This is particularly the sense of the prelude. The three succeeding movements are the diverse answers in which existence replies. . . . The fugue . . . is an expression of the reaction of life into formalism and ritualism. The succeeding movement [now the second] . . . is a comedy in the sense that Hawthorne's Celestial Railroad is a comedy.[6]

The first movement, 'maestoso' and brief, is tentative and promissory, like the hymn (Mason's *Watchman*) with which a chorus enters halfway through it: 'Watchman, tell us of the night,/ What the signs of promise are:/Traveller, o'er yon mountain's height,/See that Glory-beaming star!' Many other hymn-tune fragments are interwoven in the music, most consistently Mason's *Bethany*. Nostalgic hymn-tune passages also figure in the second, 'comedy' movement, but they are constantly being over-ridden by boisterous marches, ragtime, square-dance tunes, and patriotic ditties in phantasmagoric profusion. The stately fugue of the third movement is an orchestration, with some non-scholastic afterthoughts, of the 'Chorale' of the First String Quartet, but also with 16- and 32-foot organ pedal coloration that brings the symphony movement into relationship with the (lost) original organ version. The last movement, even more complex texturally than the second (but a tapestry of murmurs rather than shouts), calls on all the forces that have appeared variously in the preceding movements: the 'normal' orchestra (but with solo piano and voices) of the first movement, and its 'distant choir' of a few strings and harp; the very large orchestra of the second movement, with its pianos both orchestral and solo and its frequent *divisi* string parts; and the added organ of the third movement. All these are augmented in the fourth by a 'battery unit' of drums, cymbal, and gong which initiates the movement with a hushed and mysteriously intricate, anti-metric ostinato that never ceases, is wholly independent of the other music that develops around it, and fades away only after the rest of the ensemble (with humming voices) has concluded the symphony. The 'other music' around the battery unit is a gradually

[6] Quoted in John Kirkpatrick's preface to Ives's *Symphony No. 4* (New York, 1965), p. viii.

swelling complex of developments, mainly on hymn tunes previously heard, to a smiling, tranquil march, and finally a transcendent reworking of the ideas that close the Second String Quartet, with *Bethany* haloed by the distant choir.

To Bellamann's notes on the symphony Ives added a word: 'The last movement is an apotheosis of the preceding content, in terms that have something to do with the reality of existence and its religious experience' (*Memos* 66). This remark is interesting in that it implies a different way of listening to the symphony than do Bellamann's. Bellamann suggests the first movement as prelude to the following three ($1 \rightarrow 2$, 3, 4); Ives suggests the last as 'apotheosis' of the first three (1, 2, $3 \leftarrow 4$). And one may listen to the symphony as two pairs of movements, the prelude leading to the 'comedy', the fugue to the finale. Such varied possibilities for experiencing the Fourth Symphony, no one more 'correct' than another, are also available in—indeed, built into—other aspects of it besides that of gross form: tonal, timbral, textural, melodic, rhythmic.[7] In his 'Conductor's Note' for the New Music edition of the second movement (1929), Ives wrote an especially provocative statement along these lines:

As the eye, in looking at a view, may focus on the sky, clouds or distant outlines, yet sense the color and form of the foreground, and then, by bringing the eye to the foreground, sense the distant outlines and color, so, in some similar way can the listener choose to arrange in his mind the relation of the rhythmic, harmonic and other material. In other words, in music the ear may play a role similar to the eye in the above instance.[8]

He was after musical perspective and multi-dimensionality: 'As the distant hills in a landscape, row upon row, grow gradually into the horizon, so there may be something corresponding to this in the presentation of music. Music seems too often all foreground'. This multi-dimensionality of the Fourth Symphony is found in others of Ives's compositions, as we have noted, but to a lesser degree; here it is realized to the fullest.

Ives's plans for *Universe Symphony* suggest he would have carried even further such notions of multi-dimensionality. The scope

[7] As demonstrated brilliantly in William Brooks, 'Unity and Diversity in Charles Ives' *Fourth Symphony*', *Yearbook for Inter-American Musical Research*, x (1974), which deals with the first movement only.

[8] Reprinted in Ives's 'Conductor's Note', *Symphony No. 4* (New York 1965), p. 12.

of the work conceptually was enormous: it was to be 'a presentation and contemplation in tones . . . of the mysterious creation of the earth and firmament, the evolution of all life in nature, in humanity, to the Divine', as realized by a 'conclave' of groups of instruments or separate orchestras, each to have its own music, all going 'around their own orbit, [coming] to meet each other only where their circles eclipse' (*Memos* 163, 107–8). Some five to fourteen of these groups of instruments, lower-pitched, were to represent the earth; four or five, higher-pitched, were to represent the heavens; a percussion orchestra representing 'the pulse of the universe's life beat' was to underlie all. Ives had started such a work in 1915, imagining it should be played twice, 'first when the listener focusses his ears on the lower or earth music, and the next time on the upper or Heaven music' (*Memos* 106). For more than a decade he continued to make chordal and rhythmic diagrams, and more fully realized sketches, toward it and *Universe*; when dictating his *Memos* in 1932 he thought to enlarge the original piece or 'put it into the *Universe Symphony*, to which it is related'. At the same time, recognizing that he would probably not finish either, he made the ultimate offer of 'multi-dimensionality'—of Ivesian inclusiveness, humility, and generosity. In a gesture probably unprecedented among composers, he suggested (*Memos* 108) that others might like to complete his *Universe Symphony*: 'I am just referring to the above [compositional details] because, in case I don't get to finishing this, somebody might like to work out the idea'.

SELECTIVE BIBLIOGRAPHY

Cowell, Henry, and Sidney Cowell. *Charles Ives and His Music.*
New York, 1955; revised 1969.

Hitchcock, H. Wiley, and Vivian Perlis (eds.). *An Ives Celebration: Papers and Panels of the Ives Centennial Festival-Conference, 1974.* Urbana, 1977.

Ives, Charles. *Essays Before a Sonata, The Majority and Other Writings*, ed. Howard Boatwright. New York, 1961, 1962.

Ives, Charles. *Memos*, ed. John Kirkpatrick. New York, 1972.

Kirkpatrick, John. *A Temporary Mimeographed Catalogue of the Music Manuscripts and related materials of Charles Edward Ives.* New Haven, 1960; reprinted 1973.

Perlis, Vivian. *Charles Ives Remembered.* New Haven, 1974.

Rossiter, Frank R. *Charles Ives and His America.* New York, 1975.

Warren, Richard. *Charles E. Ives: Discography.* New Haven, 1972.

CORRIGENDA

The columns at the left indicate the location of asterisked matter in the text, for which corrections are given here, by page, paragraph (counting from the top of the page, even if that is in mid-paragraph), and line.

Page	Para.	Line	
5	1	3-5	John Kirkpatrick "tend[s] to gently disagree: [he] would have said Emerson."
6	3	6	But "precisely" from 1886 to 1926.
12		8	The manuscript names "Hawley, Smith, and Nevin," of whom Hawley is Charles Beach Hawley (1858-1915), but whether the Nevin is Ethelbert (1862-1901) or his brother Arthur (1871-1943) can be argued; and which of many American songwriting Smiths is not clear.
14	2	last	*Azmon* and *Woodworth* (the latter being the principal tune of the third movement)
19		1	The indications of the chords' structural basis are editorial, not Ives's nor from the published score.
21		1	Not quite "consistently"
21	2	8-9	*Rosamunde* was set first by Ives to a German text by Wilhelmine von Chézy (née Von Klencke).

Page	Para.	Line	
28		4	Ives made his "decision" in 1898.
32	3	4-5	The indications of the chords' structural basis (in Ex. 22) are editorial, not Ives's nor from the published score.
42	2	13	John Kirkpatrick thinks of the "polonaise version" as a "bolero."
66		3-4	Only the three-note segment C-B♭-A♭ is "whole-tone."
83	(Ex. 57(b))		The tune in bassoon and horn is *Naomi* ("Father, whate'er of earthly bliss"), arranged by Lowell Mason from Hans Georg Nägeli; it is very closely related to *Woodworth*.
85	1	3	(A bad slip of memory and/or the pen:) At no point in *Decoration Day* are two simultaneous marches suggested.
87	1	9	The hymn tune is *Dorrnance* ("Sweet the moments, rich in blessing"), by I. B. Woodbury. John Kirkpatrick believes that "Ives's 'later adaptation' of the music to Johnson's poem is probably a blind (he hated to divulge how his music grew)"–implying that quite possibly the texted version preceded that for orchestra.

The Institute for Studies in American Music at Brooklyn College, City University of New York, is a division of the college's Conservatory of Music. It was established in 1971. The Institute contributes to American-music studies in several ways. It publishes a series of monographs, a periodical newsletter, and special publications of various kinds. It serves as an information center and sponsors conferences and symposia dealing with all areas of American music including art music, popular music, and the music of oral tradition. The Institute also encourages and supports research by offering fellowships to distinguished scholars and, for assistance in funded projects, to junior scholars as well. The Institute supervises the series of music editions *Recent Researches in American Music* (published by A-R Editions, Inc.). I.S.A.M. activities also include presentation of concerts and lectures at Brooklyn College, for students, faculty, and the public.